How to Write
POWERFUL
COLLEGE STUDENT
RESUMES
&
COVER LETTERS

How to Write
POWERFUL
COLLEGE STUDENT
RESUMES
&
COVER LETTERS

Easy Tips, Basic Templates, Sample Formats, and
Real Examples That Get Job Interviews Like Magic

Quentin J. Schultze, Ph.D.
Bethany Kim

Foreword by
Richard N. Bolles

edenridge press

GRAND RAPIDS, MICHIGAN

MORE COLLEGE RÉSUMÉ-WRITING TIPS ONLINE
http://www.resumes4collegestudents.com

Copyright © 2010 by Quentin J. Schultze

Published by
Edenridge Press
Grand Rapids, Michigan
service@edenridgepress.com

Quantity discount pricing is available.
service@edenridgepress.com

Design: Matthew Plescher

BUS056030   BUSINESS & ECONOMICS / Careers / Résumés

ISBN 978-0-9827063-0-5 (pbk.)

Library of Congress Control Number: 2010931100
Library of Congress subject headings:
Resumes (Employment)
College students—Employment
College graduates—Employment

Acknowledgements

We are grateful for hundreds of students at Calvin College who tested the principles in this book through their informational interviews, job applications, position interviews, and classroom feedback. We also are grateful for the many internship supervisors, career development experts, employers, professors, and human resource professionals who served the students and us.

One student who merits special words of thanks is Kimberly Webster. For her senior project, she conducted a survey of college and university career development offices, and analyzed existing résumé-writing books in terms of how well they serve students.

Kim Chimienti reviewed, commented upon, and helped revise the entire manuscript. She also used the principles in this book to land a new job during dire economic times—but that's a story to be told in a follow-up book on résumé writing for new career seekers.

The "Works Cited" section of this book lists the researchers and authors from whom we learned much about the different situations, careers, contexts, and strategies for résumé and cover letter writing.

Richard N. Bolles, creator and author of the bestselling *What Color Is Your Parachute?* book series—and not a big fan of resume-writing books that overpromise and under-deliver—inspired us to ensure that our book would truly serve college students and recent graduates.

The book's design is the imaginative work of Matthew Plescher, who splendidly integrated form and content for the sake of practical usability. He's a gift to us and to readers.

We thank copyeditor Donna Huisjen, proofreader Elizabeth Banks, and indexer Lois Brom.

Tim Beals of Credo Communications facilitated everything from early brainstorming through the finished book. He knows oodles about every aspect of publishing. Tim is also an amazingly creative agent and consultant. His mind and heart are always brimming with spacious ideas.

Finally, we give thanks in advance for every person served by this book, and for everyone else who served us along the way.

Quentin J. Schultze, Ph.D.
Bethany J. Kim
Grand Rapids, Michigan USA

Contents

Works Cited

Index

Foreword

By Richard N. Bolles

Here's a puzzle for you. Why are résumés so short, and books about how to write one, so long? Why is a résumé two pages or less, while a résumé book is over 200 pages, typically? Your first guess will probably be: because a résumé gets you a job, if you do it well, so you need detailed instructions about how to do it well. Good guess; but it's wrong. A résumé's purpose is not to get you a job; it's simply to get you invited in for an interview at a place that interests you.

Okay then, your second guess might be: a résumé book has to be so long because you're essentially trying to sell yourself to an employer, and writing an effective sales-piece takes a lot of time and talent to get right. That's another good guess, but it is, again, wrong. In a sales piece, you would put in as much as possible to help would-be employers see what a splendid "catch" you would be. A good sales piece can run several pages. But in a résumé you leave out as much as possible, because the employer is reading your résumé to see if there's any excuse for screening you *out*. Put in one or two sentences too many, or mention something that you think might *eventually* "sell" you but is misinterpreted on a empty piece of paper that an employer spends about eight seconds scanning (typically), and you're toast.

All right, then, why does a solid résumé book have to be so long? To end the guessing game, I'll tell you the answer. It's because this isn't just a book about how to write a résumé. It's more than that. It's a book about how to look at yourself, how to take inventory of yourself, how to figure out what's absolutely special about you so you can gain more confidence, overcome shyness, and approach any employer not as a job-beggar, but as a prize, a treasure, who will help them more than anyone else could. *That's* why a résumé is so short, but a résumé book is so long.

You'll wonder of course, why *this* résumé book? There are dozens and dozens of them out there. What's so special about this one? Well, I'll tell you a story. I am myself an author; I've written a book that ten million people have bought. (The average book sells only 5- to 20,000 copies.) My book is a job-hunting book. You know what makes my book so popular? Before I began, I went and read every single book about job-hunting that was out there. So my book, once I wrote it, gave a job-hunter a whole bunch of books, all wrapped up in one.

This résumé book that you're holding in your hand had two authors who did exactly the same thing. They went and read every résumé book they could lay their hands on, before they sat down to write this one. That's not merely unusual; that's extraordinary. I have never read a résumé book whose authors did that. Until now. You've got a hundred books in one, here. I know all those other résumé books. So, I read this one, all the way through, page by page, to see if the authors left out anything important. They didn't. Or if they said anything I strongly disagreed with. They didn't. Or if their book was too difficult for a college student to understand. It isn't. They touched all the right bases. This book is a home run.

—Dick Bolles, author of *What Color Is Your Parachute? A Practical Manual for Job-Hunters and Career-Changers* (revised and updated annually).

Introduction
Why You Should Buy This Book

E mily showed up at my campus office. She sheepishly stuck her head in the doorway and whispered, "Dr. Schultze?"

"Hi," I replied.

"I'm Emily," she responded as we shook hands.

I could tell that Emily lacked self-confidence and probably had to overcome her own anxiety about going to see a professor she had never met.

"How may I serve you?" I asked.

Emily's Story May Well Be Your Story

Emily was a fourth-year college student who had gone through three different majors—nursing, business, and art—and was searching for a new major that would make her more marketable after graduation. Feeling pressure from parents and friends, and worried about her future, she hoped that I could help her chart a career course. To her, the future meant a real job with health benefits and enough income to pay back her college loans and free her from parental support. Emily's anxiety was obvious in her shaky voice.

"What have you been doing besides taking classes?" I asked.

"Nothing," she replied while looking out the window, avoiding eye contact.

"Really?" I wondered out loud, mildly skeptical. "What about part-time jobs, sports activities, internships, volunteering, or hobbies?"

Emily's eyes returned to mine and she offered a slight smile. "Well, I guess I've been doing a lot of things. But none of them will get me a job. I haven't done much worth putting on a résumé."

My heart went out to Emily. Like most final-year college students, she felt unprepared to enter the competitive job market. She had been putting her hopes on completing the "right" college major and earning a college degree. She assumed that somehow her professional life would eventually work out if she played by society's unspoken rules of the game: Get an education, write a résumé, get a job, and live happily ever after. Unfortunately, simple rules don't always work.

Why?

- Because economic conditions change, causing jobs and even entire career fields to come and go.

- Because earning a college degree isn't always sufficient for entering a field or getting ahead in a competitive career.

- Because new career seekers don't always know their own skills, what they really enjoy doing well (and why), and what their own life experience has already taught them.

- Because many college students wrongly believe that a résumé is just a list of former jobs and a statement of academic credentials—nothing more and nothing less.

Unless they're trained for a high-demand profession, college students and recent graduates often feel *regret* ("Why didn't I work harder in school?"), *self-doubt* ("I really don't have anything to offer the world."), and *defeat* ("Résumés only help successful people.").

Emily was one among millions of anxious career seekers. So I helped her in the same way I'll help you launch your career. I showed her how to create a "Masterlist" of her life experiences, from travel to hobbies, and from part-time work to volunteering. With my gentle encouragement, she began listing the various projects she had completed in school, the ways in which she had served her religious community, the computer technologies she knew how to use, and much more.

Emily Returns to My Office

Emily came back a week later with five pages of typewritten notes, carefully organized as bullet points by *skills* (what she could do), *knowledge* (what she knew), and *traits* (her personal qualities). This time she was even a bit upbeat. She could see on paper that she had valuable, meaningful experience, even if it wasn't full-time, paid professional work.

Before long Emily had crafted a résumé for a job in nonprofit public relations. Two months later she was employed with a county organization that helps religious groups, cities, the county, and the state coordinate services for the poor and homeless. Two years after that she joined the Red Cross in a supervisory position. Along the way she sent me e-mails, journaling her growing self-confidence, professional accomplishments, and personal satisfaction.

I'll Help You, Too

During the last 30 years I've taught the secrets of persuasive résumé writing to scores of people like Emily. Some of them were current undergraduate or graduate students. Others were recent graduates. Still others were new college graduates who had ended up in dead-end jobs. They were attending or had graduated from universities, seminaries, small private colleges, technical and art schools, and community colleges. Some had even dropped out of college and needed to find full-time employment to pay off loans and eventually re-enroll. I taught them—just as I'll teach you—how to communicate personal strengths honestly but persuasively.

I know what works on résumés and what doesn't—and why. Traditional college résumés that focus only on previous employment and academics are not usually effective. Those résumés all look and read the same. They don't give potential employers a real picture of your potential. By contrast, résumés that include relevant life experience produce results. Especially in tough economic times.

Simply stated, this book is better than others on the market for college students and recent graduates who need to generate interviews in order to get full-time work. If this were not the case, I wouldn't have spent my time writing it. I needed something better for my own students because the typical online and in-print résumé-writing material simply doesn't work. Most résumé-writing materials tend either toward hollow hype or impersonal rigidity.

So What Did I Do?

First, I started from scratch by ignoring all of the résumé-writing clichés that lack real-world proof—clichés like *never write more than one page, avoid all nonpaid work, don't refer to hobbies and life passions, list educational background first,* and on and on. It seems that everyone has an opinion about résumés but that few people actually know what works and what fails for college students and recent graduates who lack significant "paid work" experience.

Second, I reviewed all of the scientific studies about résumé writing (you'll see blurbs from these studies in this book), including those to which you can't gain access unless you have college or university privileges (this partly explains why so many of the popular résumé-writing books ignore the research and simply repeat the same old clichés).

Third, I talked to HR (human resources) experts who actually review résumés and hire college graduates at small, medium, and large for-profit and nonprofit organizations. These hardworking folks are often the gatekeepers who make the first round of cuts when stacks of résumés arrive in response to a new job posting.

Fourth, I met personally with career development staff members at numerous colleges and universities across North America to see what they have learned about résumé writing. I have the opportunity to do this frequently because I am regularly invited to speak at schools about my own communication research. I learn a lot from these highly-informed professionals who daily work with college students on interviews.

Fifth—and this is critical—I worked closely with my own junior and senior college students on developing a résumé-writing process that will lead to résumés that actually generate interviews.

What Makes This Book Unique?

You as a reader deserve to know what makes this book unique. Why should you buy this book instead of a different one? That's a fair question. Following are my major emphases in this book:

 I include *sample edits of actual résumé material* so that you can refine your language and address the most common grammatical and stylistic mistakes. You need short, direct, accurate language for an effective résumé. Look for the magnifying glass symbols.

 I summarize the key *findings of researchers* (such as psychologists and English professors) who study what works and what doesn't work when it comes to writing résumés and cover letters. Pay attention to the "Expert Advice" book symbols.

I pepper the book with *my own proven tips*—"Dr. Q's Tips"— along the way. Again, these are based on my research, experience, and interviews. I want to make sure you take them into account as you build your résumé. Keep your eyes open for the light bulb symbol.

■ I explain how to *transform your college and life experience into an effective résumé.* The truth is that you don't have to have a lot of full-time, paid *professional* experience for a solid résumé. You read that correctly. With my help, you can use your broader life experience to compose a powerful résumé that will generate job interviews. The best résumés reflect the *whole* you, not just the *worker* you.

- I teach you *the theory behind everything you should or should not include on a résumé.* That way you can truly create your own, effective résumé without just copying other people's résumé material. Once you know how to communicate through a résumé, you can impress your friends by critiquing their résumés. I'm not kidding. My students actually help their friends.

- I show you how *to tweak each résumé and cover letter for specific positions and organizations.* This is essential.

- I demonstrate *how to compose a cover letter that will immediately persuade employers to read your accompanying résumé.* In fact, the cover letter is probably the most important aspect of résumé writing. Why? Because the cover letter allows you to creatively summarize your résumé (Who wants to read a lot of résumés, anyway?) and to relate your whole-person strengths (your *skills*, *knowledge*, and *traits*) to the particular position and organization you're targeting. I'll go so far as to say that you can even get some interviews with just a well-written cover letter. Again, I'm not kidding. I'm also willing to tell you honestly that even the best résumés are usually ineffective unless they include a solid cover letter.

Do You Really Need to Buy This Book?

If you're unwilling or don't need to spend the time to write an exceptional résumé, this book is probably not for you. If you've already got the job and just need to slap together a short summary of previous jobs to satisfy the powers that be, you probably won't benefit from this book. If I were you, I wouldn't spend the money.

On the other hand, you might still want to impress your employer and prepare for future job searches or promotions. The process I describe in this book could still help you learn more about yourself, as well as about writing résumés and cover letters. Sooner or later you'll have to go through the process described in this book if you want an impressive résumé. That's why I require my college students to work through it. They're the better for it, even if they've already been accepted to graduate school or have already netted a terrific job.

The Math Is Clear

Great Résumés
+ Fine-tuned Cover Letters
Interviews

Unfortunately, as a college student or recent graduate you face a special problem: You probably don't have enough career-related experience to fill up a one-page résumé. If you recently graduated from college, you could fill in the gaps with a list of typical college courses. So what! Every other college graduate can do the same thing. Anyone can write that kind of knock-off résumé. Just fill in the blanks—when and where you worked or when and where you attended school. But no matter how many eye-popping graphics or fancy fonts you add, your résumé will probably end up at a local landfill with moldy coffee grounds and sticky stir sticks.

Get a Résumé Life

I wrote this book to show career seekers like you how to write a powerful, interview-generating résumé based on your life experience, as well as on your academic accomplishments. Even if you're only nineteen or twenty years old, you probably have plenty of life experience for documenting your skills, knowledge, and traits. You can point to hobbies, volunteer experiences, travel adventures, friendships with people from other cultures or ethnic groups, part-time jobs, self-taught skills (e.g., computer software), and self-acquired knowledge (e.g., sports, politics, media, or nature). Formal education is only part of your life story. I'll show you how to capture all of the career-related aspects of your life so that your résumé will rise to the top of the pile.

This Book Is a Calling

As I mentioned above, over the years I've tried using virtually every résumé-writing book on the market to guide new career seekers. None of them has really worked. Urged by my former students and current mentees, I wrote this book based on my proven techniques. For decades I've been receiving e-mails and phone calls from friends of friends of friends, asking me for help with their résumés. It dawned on me several years ago that I had unintentionally created a résumé-writing movement that was bigger than my ability to serve—unless I wrote a book. It was time to share my experience with people I couldn't help personally. My proven "secrets" could help many more than just my own current and former students.

In a sense, this book called me. It became one of my callings. I simply trusted that college students would discover the book and benefit from the content and inspiration. That students in their turn would be called to the book.

I didn't write this book to get rich! My wife and I donate book royalties to charitable causes, especially to college student scholarship funds. I'm blessed to have a college teaching job that I love and that helps us pay the bills. What keeps me going on book projects like this one? The grateful letters, phone calls, and e-mails from readers who are served by the words I write. It's a kind of "magic" for me to be able to help people I've never personally met.

I Needed a Coauthor

But I'm no longer a college student—to say the least.

I invited Bethany Kim to join me as coauthor because she is a more recent college graduate, a female, and a fine writer. She brings additional on-the-ground experience and keeps my writing tuned to college and post-college readers. Without her gentle prodding, I tend to become too professorial. This book connects with readers because of her persistent editing.

What Happened to Emily?

Emily eventually left public relations for graduate school to become an ESL (English as a Second Language) teacher. She also continued helping others with their résumés. I just heard from her again and discovered that she is now in a position of reviewing résumés for hiring people. She is grateful for what she learned years ago in my campus office.

My Final Plug

If you want to obtain interviews for real jobs and satisfying careers, this book is for you. If you'd like to find lines of work that match your abilities and offer room for you to grow and succeed, this is your book. Let me help you move forward by showing you how to transform your life experience into a great résumé. Result: You'll get the interview you need for the career you want.

You deserve more than an average résumé because of your invaluable life experiences. This book will show you how to transform your college and life experiences into a persuasive, interview-winning résumé. I'm honored to help you fulfill your own, special hopes and dreams. Thanks for knocking on my door!

—Dr. Q

The Naked Truths of Résumé Success

In this chapter you'll learn:

The right attitude to begin with
The right résumé-writing process to follow

I was slurping down watery spaghetti when the news reached college friends and me in the dining hall: An all-campus streak was scheduled for sunset. Dozens of female students would supposedly be dashing across the wide-open university quadrangle in their birthday suits. We quickly finished our watery Jell-O® desserts and dashed from the male dorm to the scene of the unfolding spectacle.

But before we could jostle the frantic freshmen out of the best viewing spots, the runners were already sprinting across the grassy field like proud Olympians. Alas, only a couple of females had joined the male streakers' ranks—in the middle of the pack where they couldn't be clearly eyeballed.

Of course neither I nor my inhibited friends stripped down to join the passing runners, and within 30 seconds the entire escapade was over. Observers continued shuffling around for fifteen minutes like brooding carrion birds. Then they began wandering to campus watering holes to drown their disappointments. We joined them.

As we talked it over, my friends and I realized how gullible we were. All it took was a little gossip to move us to action; within minutes, we had run like a rafter of turkeys to the campus quadrangle to gawk at

📖 *Expert Advice*

Don't Over-rely on Your Résumé

"Problems with relying too much on résumés in a job search include: (1) you might get depressed and self-critical if your résumés don't deliver a job, (2) you might get a false impression that you're seriously job-hunting just because you're sending out résumés, and (3) you might give up on your job search prematurely."

Richard N. Bolles, *What Color Is Your Parachute?*

the streakers. We wondered what we had really expected to see or to accomplish by following the other flocks of dorm guys to the much-hyped event. We'd been duped. Worse yet, we realized that we had fooled ourselves into believing something that was not likely to happen as imagined.

So it is with résumé writing. Most people fool themselves into believing they can cobble together a decent résumé and proceed to land a job. They imagine the end product—the great job—while failing to consider what they actually need to do to obtain interviews, let alone secure a job or launch a career. The same fantasies affect people in their late 20s through early 40s who hope to shift to a better career. In fact, most of us are a little like the ever-hopeful college guys or girls headed to the beach to meet Mr. or Ms. "Right." Only after we catch a glimpse of ourselves once again in the mirror at the beach house bathroom do we admit that we need to work out a bit or reenergize our dieting program if we expect to impress other sun worshippers.

One time my wife and I, in our mid-40s, accidentally ended up on one of the "great" nude beaches of the world. Even though everybody else was naked, we were not inclined to take off our suits. Neither of us had the kind of physique we wanted to flaunt. But the more we sneaked peeks at other sunbathers, the more we realized that hardly any*body* was perfect. Believe me, that beach, once featured on *Entertainment Tonight*, was hardly the stuff of an erotic landscape. It was littered with oddly shaped and out-of-shape people. As far as I could tell, everybody there needed a bit more personal discipline if they expected to impress others with their birthday suits.

What about the streakers? From what my college friends and I could tell at the time, they were just as imperfect as the beachgoers. But they had a mission; they had a purpose, however wacky. They courageously sought to undress on campus and to briskly run from point

A to point B without getting arrested for public indecency. They had even planned the whole affair secretly so that word wouldn't spread in advance among authorities, let alone among freshman males like my friends and me. By contrast, we were just fantasy-driven gawkers, mere consumers—if not voyeurs of other people's carefully planned work. So what?

So this: Most career-seeking résumé writers are like the observers at that college streak. They want the fun without the planning. They expect a free ticket to an interview based on little or no résumé-writing preparation. In consequence, they usually get what they deserve: a very disappointing "show." As the old saying goes, you get what you pay for. A rafter of turkeys will always be a bunch of birds, at least until they learn how to make something more of themselves. And it won't do any good for them to fantasize about the great life of being a bald eagle, soaring overhead and grabbing fish right out of the lake. They have to train for the job as well as desire it. Then they have to convince others that they can do the work well.

Those streakers had more than a mission. They had determination and courage. They knew the importance of collaborating with others to make the streak a success.

Here's the bottom line: Writing a great résumé is a lot like streaking. The art of streaking includes many of the same traits you'll need for writing a great résumé. Both require courage. Both can be fun. Both are a bit unconventional—if you do them well. Although hiring a professional résumé writer can help, it won't engage your own creativity and prepare you for interviews. Having someone else write your résumé is like recruiting a surrogate

Expert Advice 📖

Ponder Yourself

"Writing a résumé requires you to spend quality time thinking about who you are and the impact you've made in the past."

Julie Jansen, *I Don't Know What I Want, But I Know It's Not This*

Expert Advice 📖

Consider Your Competition: Those Already Employed

"The vast majority of those who use the Internet to gather information about employment are already employed. The Internet enables them more easily to explore other companies and careers even while holding full-time jobs."

Betsey Stevenson, "The Internet and Job Search," *The Wharton School, University of Pennsylvania* streaker to take your place. It's just not the same thing. You need to tell your own life story if you want to write a personalized, powerful résumé. You need to start with the right attitude.

Be Courageous

A lot of résumés fall flat because they aren't daring. They rely on the same old lingo to say the same old things in the same old, repetitive, tired ways. Reading them is like seeing the movie *Groundhog Day* over and over again—without the happy ending. Just look at all the résumé-writing books that tell you what to say and exactly how to say it. Or peruse all the Microsoft Word® résumé templates that give every content-weak résumé the look of every other high-on-gravy, low-on-meat résumé. Where's the beef?

Don't be afraid to emphasize your strengths and express your potential. If you don't have faith in your abilities, why should anyone else? It takes guts to go streaking. It takes nerve to create a résumé that will stand out from the pack. I'm not talking about hollow hype or puffy prose. I'm talking about honest persuasion.

We all let our self-doubts cloud even our realistic dreams. We wonder whether we're good enough, bright enough, and talented enough. We fear failure. All of us. I know. I've helped many college students write dynamite résumés. Almost all of these career seekers started with low confidence. Why? Because no one had ever helped them review the practical value of their *life* experience. They worried excessively about their lack of *professional* experience. Some of them even wanted to exaggerate part-time work experiences to make it seem as though their professional backgrounds were more substantial. That doesn't work. It's unethical as well as ineffective.

Also, we all tend to remember and dwell upon our weaknesses rather than our strengths. Every former job we list on a résumé reminds us that we didn't perform perfectly. We wonder what our confidential references will *really* say about us. Every career seeker—old or young,

📖 *Expert Advice*

Answer Want Ads within Your Résumé

"Think of the 'help wanted' ad as the question, and your résumé as the answer."

Lance Turner, *Arkansas Business*

male or female—feels inadequate. Writing a résumé can make you feel even worse if you don't know how to tell your story persuasively. Get ready. Take courage. I'll coach you.

It can take days to write a solid résumé, weeks to identify a job worth applying for, and months to land an interview. The process of launching a career can be slow and tedious. One day you'll assess yourself and your résumé as outstanding. The next day you'll want to tear it up and toss it in the trash. Sometimes you'll feel like giving up. To keep your sanity, you'll want to download entire seasons of old TV shows; go shopping; hang out at a coffee shop eating pastries; or simply sleep until noon, slurp down a can of unheated *SpaghettiOs*®, and then crawl back into bed. Don't let yourself cop out. Short breaks are okay. Just don't avoid the inevitable. Steel yourself for a long and bumpy road. Take courage!

Frustrations can devour you if you let them. It may be that 95 percent of the time you've put into applications and résumés has lead to *nothing. Nada.* You've faced the dreaded black hole of submitted résumés. You haven't even received a form letter saying, "Sorry, but no." It's infuriating.

If you're new to the job-search process, you should expect to be ignored by some employers, no matter how great your résumé and cover letter may be. That's just the way things are, so don't take it personally. But you can greatly increase your employer response rate and interviews by following the tips in this book. So take courage, even if you've been beaten down in the past.

Be Creative

Creating a résumé really can be enjoyable. You get to be imaginative. You can paint a self-portrait with words, tell your own story, make your case with style.

Expert Advice

Prove Yourself

"Your work and other activities provide material for you to write concrete 'proof statements' on résumés and in cover letters. They can demonstrate to potential employers that you 'possess experiences and skills necessary for success.'"

Karl L. Smart, "Articulating Skills in the Job Search: Proving by Example," *Business Communication Quarterly*

Dr. Q's tip

Think of the "job" of writing your résumé as a chance to persuade others that, given a chance, you can do terrific work for them. Not that you have all of the sought-after *professional* experience. Rather, show that you've got *life* experience. You're walking, talking potential just waiting to be tapped by a wise employer. Don't slip into arrogance or a cocky attitude. Do gain self-confidence from your life experience.

As I discuss in this book, one way to liven up résumés is with applied creativity. Search for just the right words to describe your *skills*, *knowledge*, and *traits* (these are the "big three" we'll talk much more about later). Describe some personal activities that are interesting and will catch a reader's attention—perhaps hobbies or adventurous travel, a passion for reading mysteries or for learning everything you can about particular sports teams or players. What excites you? Why?

How would you tell someone else about your passions? What words would you use? Right now, stop and think about one thing you like doing when you have free time. What does that activity say about you? Start thinking outside the box.

Suppose you like eating. Why? Is it the taste—the *variety* of flavors? Do you enjoy different food experiences? Going out to eat? Eating with others? Cooking your food and then eating it? When, why, where, and with whom you eat can say a lot about you.

I've noticed that many people who love to eat are great conversationalists. They enjoy interacting, listening to others' stories, and sharing their own life adventures: "You'll never guess what happened to me last week at the car wash—I accidentally left the passenger-side window open." They're schmoozers, tailor-made for conversation-rich careers. Their creativity comes with expressing their schmooze power in a way that highlights the strengths they offer a potential employer: an "avid conversationalist who builds relationships by listening and speaking well." Sounds like a salesperson. Or a teacher. Perhaps even a résumé-book author!

Expert Advice

Balance Work and Personal Entries

"Strike a balance between listing work achievements and listing personal information about yourself."

Jim Bright and Joanne Earl, *Brilliant CV: What Employers Want to See and How to Say It*

Maybe you did something special while engaged in a run-of-the-mill, part-time job. What was *your* contribution to enhancing the value of the mundane tasks? How did you serve your coworkers or customers? How did you brighten someone else's day even in a routine job? How did you transform an everyday task into a more bearable one—besides quitting? If you did resign, what positive statement does this action make about your ethical standards? Or about your patience or loyalty for hanging in there for so long?

We all need to get the work done, but *why* and *how* we work is just as important as *what* we accomplish. After all, few jobs are solo efforts. Would you rather work with a dull or a fun colleague? If you were hiring someone for a sales position, would you prefer a conversationalist or a quiet loner? What about for a library job? When it comes to résumé writing, one size does *not* fit all situations. You need to know what you personally have to offer and under what circumstances those qualities might be a good fit.

Get your creative juices flowing in the following chapters. Imagine yourself writing a poem, crafting a playlist of your favorite songs, snapping a series of photos, filming your life story, or painting an image of who you are and who you would like to become. Don't start by imagining yourself in a professional suit. If it helps, peel off some clothes late at night and roam unencumbered around your living quarters. Just make sure the blinds are drawn, or you might end up telling your tale creatively to the authorities.

Be Unconventional

It may sound obvious, but there's only one you. You should be yourself in your résumé. You can borrow good ideas from other résumés. But remember that overly standardized, run-of-the-mill résumés tend to get tossed into the recycle bin. Who wants to employ an imitation if they can hire the real thing?

In highly creative professions, especially the arts, conventional résumés are nearly useless. But even in less-artsy fields like accounting and computer science, cookie-cutter résumés are less effective. With a boring, predictable résumé, even someone with fabulous life experience can resemble a tasteless, manufactured cookie rather than a

Expert Advice

gooey one hot out of the oven. Go for the goo! How? By expressing what makes you distinctive. What captures your own life recipe.

In short, *you* are a distinctive member of the human race. An engaging résumé should capture your individuality, even as it conforms to some of the tried-and-true basics of a professional résumé for a particular career. In other words, be innovative within the parameters of professionalism. This will make you deliciously unconventional in a world of knock-off career seekers who wrongly believe that imitation itself is a résumé-writing virtue.

Of course, avoid extreme or inappropriate individuality. Elle Woods in the movie *Legally Blonde* uses a pink, scented résumé. Cute, but it won't make a good impression in most professions. Avoid the extremes even if you truly are *that* unconventional.

So use this book to discover your own exceptional traits. Then express those traits creatively, within the accepted rules of résumé writing.

Be Vulnerable

Sending out résumés can be humiliating. You might not hear anything back, making you wonder whether either *you* or the *employer* is a loser. Or you might snag an interview and then be asked tough questions about your résumé, causing you to fret over your weaknesses. Just writing a résumé can be embarrassing if it seems as though you've got so little professional experience that you're unworthy of employers' attention.

Like streaking, or even like sunbathing on a nude beach, letting other people see who you are, warts and all, is humbling and sometimes embarrassing. We all crave acceptance. We need to know that others value us for who we are. But we fear being rejected if we're honest about ourselves. Feeling this way is normal for people of all ages. Deep inside we're all like teenagers going through identity crises. A friend of mine who makes movies says that working in Hollywood is like living in purgatory with a bunch of adolescents. Truth be told, there's a lot of the insecure Hollywood celeb in all of us. We all protect ourselves by projecting personas in order to mask our inner doubts and fears.

Done properly, preparing your résumé can help you to come out of your overly protective shell. It can actually encourage you to accept and express your strengths, as well as to identify and address your weaknesses. One of my former colleagues faced a real challenge teaching public speaking: Students tended to cut class on the day they were expected to stand up and explain to their peers one thing they could do well. Either they couldn't identify any area of proficiency (unlikely) or were simply embarrassed about revealing it to others.

Use your résumé writing as a way to remind yourself that you're unique, that your life experience has already taught you volumes, and that your experience itself qualifies you to tell others about your strengths and to address your self-identified weaknesses as opportunities for growth. If you do, employers will pick up on your distinctiveness, your self-confidence, and your desire to learn from your life experience. Smart employers don't look for perfect people to interview. They look for honest, mature individuals who know their own strengths and weaknesses and are willing to continue learning. But to get there you'll need to lower your defenses.

If the real you doesn't speak persuasively in your résumé, you probably don't yet have a great one. Your résumé needs to reveal your career-related skills, knowledge, and traits in order to make a case for your career potential. By revealing the value of your own life experience, you'll be making a strong case for the kind of employee you'll make—not just for the type of career you'd like to launch.

Be Organized

Let me be frank: The greatest weakness I see in college students today is disorganization. Students are busily hopping from one project to the next one, which was due yesterday. They're trying to juggle academics, relationships, jobs, finances, and everything else that can turn their

📖 *Expert Advice*

Ask How Your Résumé Compares

"It pays to ask a career counselor, professor, or other professional to review your résumé before circulating it. Ask them, 'How does mine compare with those of other students you've worked with? Be brutally honest with me—will it compete with the best?'"

Peter Vogt, *Career Wisdom for College Students*

college experiences into a rat race. Teachers often contribute to the problem by assigning a lot of busywork.

Also, colleges don't do a very good job of teaching students basic life-organization skills. College students end up working on the next assignment due rather than organizing and scheduling their work for maximum efficiency and effectiveness.

The same thing happens with résumés. As you probably already know firsthand, students tend to compose résumés and cover letters at the last minute. This leads to poorly written and even error-riddled material that creates a poor impression. Moreover, last-minute résumé writing never maximizes the value of academic and life experience. It leads to copycat résumés and cover letters that might be visually attractive but lack persuasive power.

This book provides a simple but powerful process for writing your own interview-generating résumés and cover letters. If you follow this process you'll be successful.

On the following page is a basic flow chart for the process I will develop throughout the rest of the book. I've included it as appendix I as well. Appendix H is a "Résumé Checklist" that you can use to make sure you've addressed every step in the flow chart.

This straightforward organizational process outlines specific action steps along the way. The chapters that follow are filled with concrete examples, checklists, and sample résumé excerpts. Take heart. But also do what I say. Work at it. Steadily. Committedly. Step by step. Stay organized.

The job-search process can become one of the most challenging aspects of your life. Sure, paying bills, watching friends leave town, getting married or divorced, and caring for children or parents can all be enormously stressful. But in one sense, nothing else compares to job hunting. Why? Because without income we will lack the resources

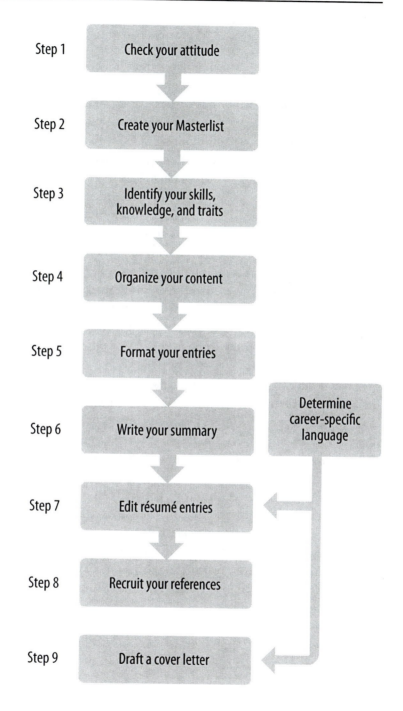

Step 1	Check your attitude
Step 2	Create your Masterlist
Step 3	Identify your skills, knowledge, and traits
Step 4	Organize your content
Step 5	Format your entries
Step 6	Write your summary
Step 7	Edit résumé entries
Step 8	Recruit your references
Step 9	Draft a cover letter

Determine career-specific language

📖 *Expert Advice*

Save Job Descriptions

"Retain copies of descriptions of formerly held positions so that you can refer to that language appropriately in relevant résumés."

Stephen Jones, "How to Create a Winning Résumé," *The Black Collegian*

to address any of the other aspects of life. Whether we like it or not, launching a first or a new career is a competitive task. Any of us could survive by cobbling together days, weeks, and months of various go-nowhere part-time jobs. But if we want to flourish, if we seek a real, meaningful career, we have to learn how to sell ourselves persuasively, even if we lack significant or specific professional experience.

What's the alternative? Flipping a few burgers at night and watching endless infomercials on daytime TV? Nursing one cold cup of coffee for hours on end while reading and rereading the local entertainment weekly at a nearby java joint? Searching for a wealthy significant other? Mooching off parents or friends—or even children— until they boot us out? These activities might help if you're a novelist looking for material. They won't lead you to a powerful résumé and a persuasive cover letter.

You'll have to put hours—perhaps even days—into preparing résumés and cover letters that some potential employers still might not even look at seriously. Unless you happen to be in one of the few high-demand fields, employers don't need *you*. You need *them*. You have to get their attention and win them over without coming across as an egotistical careerist bent on saving employers from their ignorance.

If you're new to career hunting, get ready to receive rejections. Sometimes an inside candidate will already have the job you're applying for. Sometimes the human relations office will have its favorites in spite of what other staff members may tell you. You'll get down on yourself. You might even feel as though you don't really have anything to offer. Nonsense! You just need help transforming your life experience into persuasive potential.

I hope you have instant success with the first résumé you send out. Realistically, though, you'll need to work hard. Now you know the naked truth. So let's get started.

Conclusion

Writing a résumé begins with the right attitude. It takes courage, creativity, unconventionality, vulnerability, and organization. Following the right steps—carefully and completely—is critically important. The rest of this book takes you through the necessary steps. But you've got to start off with a positive, adventurous attitude. No one wants to interview, let alone hire, a self-critical, boring, or boastful individual. Your beginning attitude will influence everything you do to get a job, including your résumé and cover letter.

What to Do Now

Take a few deep breaths. Relax. Think about all the things in your life for which you're thankful. Then visualize one more gift—*you*. And your life experience. Once you recognize your own value as a distinctive person, you're ready to begin to positively express who you are to others. You're ready to graduate to chapter 2.

Where to Begin

In this chapter you'll learn:

What a résumé really is
How to get your name and numbers right
Why life experience is so important

I was giving a presentation to college students about résumé writing when all of a sudden a group in the back of the room started chatting, making it difficult for others in the classroom to hear me. I paused my presentation and waited. Everyone in the room was now staring at the yappers. Finally, the chatterers realized they had become the center of attention, smiled at me, straightened up, and became extremely attentive—as though nothing had just occurred.

Given my innate curiosity, I couldn't let the situation pass without a question. "Did I say something that sparked your conversation?" I asked the now-attentive group. Smiles. Silence. Awkwardness for all of us in the room. Then a reply from one group member, "Yes, Dr. Schultze. We were just talking about the fact that we wish we could redo the résumés we sent out last week. Based on what you were saying a few minutes ago, we think we made some mistakes."

"Like what?" I asked.

"Like our phone numbers. We used our dormitory numbers, and we won't be living there in six weeks," offered a second participant from the talkers' group.

"Yeah, and I used my mobile phone number, which is going to change when I graduate and move to Florida next month," chimed in another concerned student. "We're trying to figure out what to do. Should we send out corrections?"

Believe it or not, this kind of scenario gets replayed over and over again during my résumé-writing workshops. Why? Because the most essential parts of a résumé—the name and contact information—are taken for granted. Everyone wants to focus on the "meat" of their résumé, so they slap their name, address, phone number, and e-mail address on the top of the page and never reconsider that information until one of those items becomes obviously outdated. Then they revise it with the same perfunctory attitude. A number is a number—right? A name is a name—correct?

No. Résumé names and numbers define who you are in potential employers' eyes. They also direct potential interviewers to you, just as a yellow pages listing gives a potential customer an impression of a local business and informs the community about where and how to contact the company. When I get an "out of service" message in response to a quick call to the plumber, I don't start researching the company to determine whether it has moved or changed phone numbers. I just look for a different plumber. I figure the company is either out of business or does a lousy job of serving customers, since it could have left a forwarding message on the old phone number for six months or a year—until new phone books come out and online directories are updated.

So how do you serve *your* customers—*your* potential employers? What kind of employer-friendly image do you project? For how long will human relations departments be able to find you after you send out a batch of résumés? Think about this: What would happen if an organization suddenly found your résumé in a file of "past applicants" six months after you had submitted it? The college students in my workshop were rightly beginning to ponder these questions. They were starting to face the reality of writing a résumé for a career rather than just a short-term job. Now it's your turn to do the same, beginning with the most important issue, the one to which nearly everyone *thinks* they know the answer—the nature of a résumé.

What's a Résumé?

U.S. Supreme Court Justice Potter Stewart once said that although he couldn't define pornography, he knew it when he saw it. The same holds true for résumés. You probably know one when you see one. But can you define one? Do you know what really makes a résumé a résumé? Do you know how employers think about and use résumés? Knowing a résumé when *you* see one isn't sufficient. More pertinent is how employers identify a great or a poor résumé when they see one.

As I stated earlier, an authentic résumé is far more than a list of jobs. A résumé is "you" in a particular written format. A résumé is "you" on paper or on a computer screen. A résumé is what you offer to an employer—somewhat like what a restaurant menu offers its customers. Of course, there are fast-food menus that let customers buy exactly the same burger at every chain restaurant. But many restaurants aren't selling generic burgers. And customers don't want any old burger. Unless they're so hungry they just need something to wolf down, they want to know what the burger is like and what comes with it—size, sauce, bun, garnishes, flavorings, etc. The "fast-food" type companies often need a worker quickly for a limited time, and they rightly hire through temporary agencies. I assume you're looking for more than a temporary position, so you need more than a fast-food menu of your abilities. Your résumé is like your personal, specialized menu of what you offer your customers—your potential employers.

Here's a definition:

Your résumé is a short (one- or two-page), outlined, persuasive presentation of your potential to contribute to the success of a particular type of organization.

Expert Advice

Anticipate Minority Bias

"If you're a minority student, express your personal information in ways that will not trigger unfavorable stereotypes. Sensitive information could include how you state your name and what you emphasize as extracurricular activities."

Barbara D. Davis and Clive Muir, "Résumé Writing and the Minority Student," *Business Communication Quarterly*

One or Two Pages

A résumé is *one or two pages* long, depending upon the situation and how much career-related information you actually have. Some employers preach that a career seeker—and especially an inexperienced applicant—should NEVER, EVER use a two-page résumé. Based on my decades of experience helping career seekers, however, I can attest that most employers are flexible. They don't like puffed-up, overwritten, unfocused résumés and resent wasting their time reading lengthy, generic résumés that could be used to apply for any job in any of numerous fields. But most employers appreciate a one- or a two-pager that includes the "right stuff," aimed at a specific career or organization.

Dr. Q's tip

Write both a one-page and a two-page résumé for each career of interest so you have them both available for last-minute revisions.

So the important things are that your résumé contains relevant, concisely written material and that it emphasizes what you can do for the organization (not what the organization can do for you). Evaluate every single one of your potential employment opportunities to determine what kinds of material to include or exclude. When in doubt, ask a couple of people who work in that field to review your résumé ahead of time—with and without the material about which you're uncertain. If *they* say your résumé is too long or too detailed, cut out the less relevant material and go with one page. In any case, don't begin writing a résumé with length in mind. Instead, think *relevance, conciseness*, and *service*. You can always pare down your résumé for specific applications or interviews.

Outline

Think of a résumé as a sentence *outline*, not a wordy essay or a fancy design template. In other words, think in terms of facts, descriptions, and events—what you did, why you did it, when you did it, and what you learned by doing it. You're reporting about your life. Since no one else has lived your life, your outline is going to be different from everyone else's. If it's not, your résumé is too generic—a dry, tasteless burger with nothing on it. You don't have to use bullet points on your résumé, but for now think in terms of a list of bulleted sub-points under each résumé entry.

Persuasive Presentation

A résumé is a *persuasive presentation*, not a bunch of bland job tidbits, a predictable list of completed college courses, a string of past jobs, or a haven for hollow hype. Your résumé should promote you honestly and convincingly by documenting your paid and nonpaid life experiences as they relate to a particular career and even to a specific job or organization. The facts you select and how you state those facts become your case for why you should be interviewed.

Although your résumé is essentially an outline, it must tell *your* story—and tell it in a *relevant* manner. Of course, not everything in your life will be pertinent to a specific job. So you have to decide which chapters from your life story will most effectively persuade potential employers. You get to persuade readers partly by editing and emphasizing particular events from your life story. Your goal is to attract the employers' attention and get them hooked on interviewing you. Your résumé should persuade the employer to want to talk with you in person. Then you'll get to tell your story even more fully and persuasively to your interviewers.

While researching the market for this book, my coauthor and I perused at least 30 different résumé books. An alarming number of them contain only about 25 percent useful material, along with 75 percent generic résumés. This would have been acceptable if the résumés in these tomes were interesting, engaging, and well written. Instead, most of them include a bland objective statement ("Objective: Entry level job in …"), along with a boring list of

Expert Advice 📖

Female Accountant Résumés

"In Big-Five accounting jobs, company recruiters rank entry-level female candidates with two-page résumés more highly than those with one-page résumés."

Elizabeth Blackburn-Brockman and Kelly Belanger, "One Page or Two?: A National Study of CPA Recruiters' Preferences for Résumé Length," *Journal of Business Communication*

Expert Advice 📖

Tell Your Story

The process of creating your résumé "may be more important than the result of that process. You will learn how to tell your story."

Dan Miller, *48 Days to the Work You Love*

college classes and wordy paragraphs about previous jobs. They read like dictionary entries. Or, worse yet, like an online or printed telephone directory entry in the white pages. Instead, make your résumé interesting (without being gimmicky) by highlighting who you are and what you offer. The last thing you want is for your potential employer to reach for your résumé because he's run out of sleep aids. Are you really that dull? If so, you need a life, not just a career!

℘ *Résumé Excerpt*

Outlining

Founder and Chair, Arragon University International Business Club, Vancouver, BC (20XX)
- Launched campus organization for students to learn about international business through lectures by and discussions with business leaders
- Selected, invited, and hosted club's first four speakers

Unless you have three or more sub-points, for most résumé entries use bullets to document sub-points on a résumé, beginning each new point with an action verb that persuasively delineates what you have actually done.

Seriously, don't let the fact that a résumé is essentially an outline color your view of who you are and what you have to offer an employer. The outline is the *form*, not the *content*. You're the interesting person behind the résumé. As you'll soon discover, you can portray your personality by using the right language, especially through the use of action verbs. Employers will be able to "see" you doing what your résumé says you *have* done, *are* doing, and *plan to* do on their behalf.

"Sells" Your Potential

A great résumé "sells" your *potential*, based on your past experiences and achievements. Remember that employers usually have to consider the likely future benefits of hiring you over any other applicant. What's in it for them if they hire you over someone else? Your résumé gives you a chance to leverage your life experiences, to highlight what you can contribute to an organization's (and your supervisor's) success. Employers who review your résumé are looking for the kind of *person* who will make them look good. They care about the whole you, not just about one or another skill you may possess. If they don't, you might not want to work for them anyway. Their company is probably not the kind of place that will help you transform a job into a career.

The secret behind every great career seeker's résumé is relevant persuasiveness. Knowing *what* to include in a résumé and *how* to express it are both critically important. Your job is to include those entries that will highlight three relevant things about you. These are what I call the "Big Three." Memorize them now. If you need a memory aid, try "SKiT." These are your "lines" for your own résumé skit:

1. Your *skills* (what you can do)
2. Your *knowledge* (what you know)
3. Your *traits* (your personality, the kind of person you are)

Throughout this book I'll show you how to develop a terrific résumé based on these three foundational elements. For now, remember that skills, knowledge, and traits are distinct, though related. Avoid thinking only in terms of the first category, skills. A dozen job applicants might have the same skills, but only one of them might know *why* and *when* to use a given skill—the latter person's *knowledge* is a critical advantage. Moreover, perhaps only one applicant possesses the right traits to apply the skills and knowledge, while working with particular kinds of people in a specific type of organization. Combined with even basic skills or knowledge, personal traits can be especially relevant and particularly persuasive.

The Big Three aspects of your life story—your skills, knowledge, and traits—are the keys to transforming your life experience into a

⚲ *Résumé Excerpt*

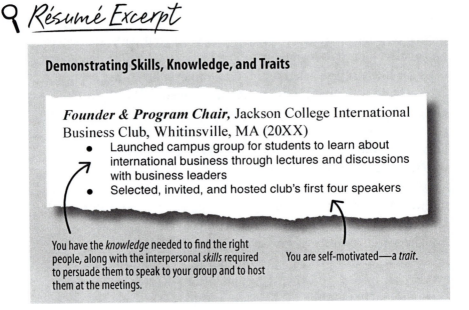

Demonstrating Skills, Knowledge, and Traits

Founder & Program Chair, Jackson College International Business Club, Whitinsville, MA (20XX)
- Launched campus group for students to learn about international business through lectures and discussions with business leaders
- Selected, invited, and hosted club's first four speakers

You have the *knowledge* needed to find the right people, along with the interpersonal *skills* required to persuade them to speak to your group and to host them at the meetings.

You are self-motivated—a *trait*.

standout, interview-generating, career-opening résumé. Why? Because every employee is a person, not just a worker. And because employers seek employees who have the right combinations of skill, knowledge, and personality. Employers ask themselves: "What can this person do for us?" "What does he or she know?" "Is this the type of person we want to work with—or who will interact well with our clients or customers?" "Does this applicant offer life knowledge and a winning attitude—not just the desired skills?"

While I'm writing this book, one of my closest mentors is trying to decide what to do about two of her highly skilled but hopelessly critical employees. She's been dealing with these two naysayers for over a year. They're continuously bad-mouthing colleagues, gossiping about office politics, and challenging their supervisors' decisions. Yet they are really talented at

📖 *Expert Advice*

Underscore Your Self-Financed Education

"You can demonstrate the trait of 'personal initiative' by indicating that you personally financed all or part of your education."

Beverly Culwell-Block and Jean Anna Sellers, "Résumé Content and Format—Do the Authorities Agree?" *Bulletin of the Association for Business Communication* working with customers. Yesterday my mentor became my mentee; she asked *me* for advice about what to do with these two misguided employees, even though I *know* very little about her business and even less about the *skills* required for doing the work well. I do, however, have experience working with people with all kinds of *personality* traits. My advice? Kindly show those two employees the door so that they can apply their skills and employ their vast store of knowledge in the right kind of setting. Help them find a more fitting career position. Then everyone will be happier. Square pegs can never be retrofitted for round holes.

Dr. Q's tip

If you don't have specific, job-required skills, you need to demonstrate on your résumé that you:

already have similar skills that could easily be transferred to a specific job and eventually a career,

or

that you have the kinds of personality traits that demonstrate your ability to pick up the needed skills quickly and well.

Both the organization and the two employees are being poorly served by the current matchup. The employees gossip about colleagues and undermine the company because they're unhappy, frustrated, and stressed out. They feel as though they have to make others look bad so they can look good—even though they're remarkably talented. They would probably flourish in a setting with less stress and less emphasis on teamwork. Well, that was my advice about these troubled and troubling employees—again, even though I wasn't qualified to address their career-specific skills and knowledge.

Most organizations today recognize that the Big Three are all critically important in the interviewing, hiring, and employee review processes. Résumé writers who persuasively address all three stand a much greater chance of being taken seriously as viable candidates. We all serve others with our whole selves, not just with our skills *or* our knowledge *or* our traits.

All else being equal, these three keys, when matched with the right organization, will open the door for interviews. There are simply too many "equals" out there for you to ignore the reality of "whole person" (holistic) hiring. Imagine all of the college students who have similar degrees from similar schools, where they have lived in similar dorms,

📖 *Expert Advice*

Make the First Cut

"Employers first review résumés to determine who is worth interviewing, not to hire. One software development manager says that he initially sorts résumés on the basis of passion, pickiness, English, brains, selectivity (that you focused deeply on something), hard-core (e.g., you're really into technology), and diversity (breadth of experience)."

Joel Spolsky, *Smart and Gets Things Done: Joel Spolsky's Concise Guide to Find the Best Technical Talent*

sipped similar types of coffee in order to stay awake in similar classes, earned credit for similar internships, joined similar student organizations, and achieved similar grades. As a career seeker, whether or not you're a college student, you need to set yourself apart from the "similar" pack with an outstanding, personal, life experience-based résumé. You need to persuade via your knowledge and traits as well as your skills.

In some situations knowing how to gain skills is more important than already possessing specific skills. Why? Because organizations occasionally assume that it will take more time and effort to retrain a new employee than to train them from scratch in particular ways to use those skills. For years I helped former students shift from newspaper advertising copywriting to broadcast media copywriting. It was almost always the same issue for radio and TV media: Could someone trained in print writing also write for the TV "eye" or for the radio "ear" (the "theatre of the mind")? Some accomplished newspaper writers could make the shift. Others never could.

Then the Internet came along and created some wonderfully mind-expanding, skill-transferring, career-building opportunities for people from all of these media (including skilled writers who were also closet "techies" with a love for computer programming).

A skill is never just one skill. It never has been. Economies and jobs change. Skilled people adapt. Wise employers know which skill sets to look for that might transfer well to emerging positions in new types of work. Skills morph.

But one essential skill in almost all of work and life is the ability to put yourself in someone else's shoes. To see reality through another person's eyes. To become skilled at one specific character trait: empathy. In fact, writing a career-launching or career-changing résumé is partly an act of empathizing with potential employers. From the very top of the résumé, the very first line, you need to demonstrate your ability and desire to put yourself in the employers' shoes. That starts with your name and numbers.

Get Your Name and Numbers Right

- Spell your name correctly. No kidding. I've seen names misspelled because résumé writers just assumed they had typed their names correctly and never checked to make sure. I've done it myself on letters and e-mails. Hardly anything is more embarrassing on a résumé. Imagine that you're the employer and you find that an applicant's name is spelled differently on the résumé than in the cover letter. How would you feel about that applicant?

- Avoid chummy nicknames. "Jack" is okay for John. "Pete" is fine for Peter. But don't use "Natster" for Nate or Nathaniel. Even if you want all of your friends and coworkers to call you "Butch" or "Sammy" (for Samantha), use your formal, given name on your résumé. My legal name is Quentin, so I always use it on résumés, applications, and business cards, even though friends call me "Quin," "Q," or "Dr. Q." Informalities are great for hanging out, but not for writing résumés. Respect your formal name. Employers will respect you for using it. When you meet potential employers, you can invite them to use your nickname if it's appropriate for a professional setting: "Glad to meet you. I'm Cynthia Smith, but please call me 'Cindy.'"

- Use a middle initial, especially if your first and last names are relatively common. A middle initial helps to individualize your résumé as your own life story. It also says that you respect formalities and legalities. If your first and last names are extremely common (e.g., James Smith or Susan Jones), you should use your full middle name. Think about it this way:

What name would you use on a business card that you hope to still be using ten years from now? Think distinguished future career, not present friends. Think business card, not Facebook. Be sure to use the same full name on LinkedIn.com.

■ Include other personal designations or titles only if they are necessarily distinctive or professionally important because you have used them in the past or intend to use them in the non-immediate future. These include such designations as "Jr.," "II," "Hon.," certification or credential designations, and significant educational degrees that are not always necessary in a field and thus set you apart (such as "BSN" for Bachelor of Science in Nursing).

Don't overdo your name! Here's the ultimate in mind-numbing, résumé-hyping madness:

Mr. Lawrence E. J. "Mac" MacArthur Jr. III, Esq., B.S.

This kind of nuttiness screams "ARROGANT!" Keep your name simple, straightforward, and appropriate rather than excessively formal.

After putting your name at the top of the résumé, list your contact information—the "numbers" interested parties will need in order to get and stay in touch with you, even if they don't respond to your résumé immediately. You never know how long your past résumés will be floating around various offices and sitting in digital databases awaiting retrieval. Therefore, you need to specify where you'll be and how you can be tracked down in both the near and not-so-immediate future.

This is especially important in seasonal hiring and in economically sensitive careers. For instance, if a teacher leaves mid-year, a school principal or superintendent will review on-file résumés in the hope of making a fairly quick hiring decision. In advertising, jobs tend to come and go with the economy. Similarly, sales opportunities can rise and fall with the fortunes of particular companies and product lines. My point is that employers often maintain files of possible candidate résumés to review as needed. This is why it's essential to include long-term as well as short-term contact information on your résumé.

In most cases you'll need to submit your résumé along with a cover letter (more on this later) explaining how you heard about the position and why you're the ideal candidate for it. Even though you include contact information in the letter, you should add it to your résumé as well. Cover letters and résumés sometimes get separated in offices and on computers. If you decide to use a header with your name on the top of a two-page résumé, don't include the header on the first page (just like for page numbers).

If you're currently a student, chances are you don't know for certain where you'll be living, let alone working, in a year or two. So you have two options: (1) Create semi-permanent contact information, such as a longer-term e-mail address, phone number, and postal address (usually a stable relative's location), or (2) create a new kind of résumé to self-destruct in both paper and digital formats, leaving no trace of your existence. While the second option might be great if you're trying to replace the latest James Bond actor, the first option is more realistic. And it's simple to accomplish: Use your parents', mature siblings', or in-laws' postal address, a Web-based e-mail address (e.g., a "Gmail" account) that forwards to your changing work or school e-mail accounts, and, if possible, telephone and fax numbers that will be maintained longer by professional-sounding friends or family-related businesses.

Be sure to avoid the following kinds of e-mail addresses:

- Non-professional-sounding ones (e.g., "coolstud@" and "hotchick@")

- Cryptic, anonymous ones (e.g., "17648he" and "sJgB2O")

Resume Excerpt

Formatting temporary and longer-term contact information at the top of your résumé

Bethany J. Biker

3201 Hamstra Blvd.
Planer, PA 18032
(777) 777-7777 (cell)
person@permanentaddress.net

This is for a fairly permanent set of numbers.

Bethany J. Biker

3201 Hamstra Blvd. Planer, PA 18032 (610) 777-7777 person@permanentaddress.net

This format saves a couple of lines of precious résumé space but is harder to format cleanly. Beware of the spacing between items. It has to be sufficient to avoid having the line look like one crammed-together sentence.

Bethany J. Biker

3201 Hamstra Blvd.
Planer, PA 18032
(610) 777-7777 (cell)
person@permanentaddress.net
(permanent)

1222 Schipma Hall McCloskey University
Feyen, MD 20520
person@mcuniversity.edu
(through 5/XX)

Note that you don't need to add a telephone number to the temporary information if you have a more permanent landline or cell phone.

- Confusing zero with the letter O (e.g., "JamesO" vs. "James0") and vis versa

Here are some additional problems to avoid:

- P.O. boxes or private rental boxes that suggest impermanency

- International postal addresses that might not be reliable or might have excessively slow delivery (most military addresses with domestic addresses are exceptions)

- Incomplete phone numbers (such as numbers that lack area codes, direct office extensions, or full international dialing codes)

Dr. Q's tip

> If your word processor automatically adds underlines to e-mail and Web addresses, turn off the hyperlink feature to remove them unless you are submitting a Word or PDF résumé in which you want active links. The hyperlink underlines are inappropriate for paper résumés.

- Fax numbers that require someone to call ahead to ask the fax operator to turn on the fax machine (unprofessional)

- Phone numbers that lead to silly or inappropriate voice mail messages ("I'm not here right now because I'm out partying….")

- Business phone numbers or e-mail addresses for places where you currently work—unless you have the permission of your current employer(s)

Consider including the following in your résumé:

- A phonetic spelling of your last name if it isn't easy to pronounce correctly. I include this on my résumé and website: "The 'e' in 'Schultze' is silent." This puts at ease those who have to call me on the phone or introduce me to others. I, too, feel awkward phoning someone who has a last name I'm unsure about pronouncing correctly.

- A more permanent, dedicated fax number from one of the online services that provides a fax-only phone number (these businesses convert the incoming fax to a computer image file and send it to your e-mail address as an attachment), so that you don't need to have a landline phone in order to receive a fax. Fax machines are an old-fashioned technology in the age of computer scanning and e-mail attachments, but businesses and nonprofit organizations still use them extensively.

Recall Your Stories

After providing a complete, professional name and semi-permanent contact information, a great résumé begins delineating your relevant life experience, not just your paid jobs. Each of your life experiences is a story that says something about you. Before you start filling in your résumé, you'll need to list and describe your life experiences in terms of the Big Three (your SKiT). At this stage, don't leave even seemingly insignificant experiences off your list. You might discover later that an ostensibly irrelevant experience was the perfect lead-in for an unexpected job opportunity. You'll also discover that life experiences are excellent material for helping you to concretely answer interview questions. Your life experiences are concrete stories that you can use to teach others about yourself.

A graduating college student who had grown up near the college asked me to look over her résumé before she sent it to prospective employers. One item caught my eye. In a category labeled "additional activities" she indicated that she had helped care for her invalid mother at home throughout her college career. I asked her why she had included this on her résumé.

"I could've gone away to college, but I stayed at home in order to care for my dying mother," she began. "I guess my mom was a big part of my college education. Instead of just studying in a library cubicle, I taught myself well by explaining to her what I was studying in school. My mom never had a chance to attend college. By the time she died, she probably deserved my college degree just as much as I did."

As an employer, how would you respond to an item on a résumé that covered such a care-giving experience? This student's unique experience probably equipped her with relevant skills, knowledge, and traits for many possible careers. She was simultaneously a learner, a teacher, caregiver, and a friend. I can think of an array of fields and professions, as well as organizations, that might welcome her as a valuable employee, among them nursing, education, counseling, sales, customer service, ministry, sports training, and many more. What traits did her experience cultivate? Patience? Compassion? Empathy? Unselfishness? Depending upon the position she is applying for, she should probably document briefly on her résumé the ways in which this experience positively shaped her character.

What kinds of life experiences do you look back on fondly? What gave you satisfaction at work or at play? What did those experiences teach you about yourself? About the skills, knowledge, or traits that would equip you to serve a potential employer?

Answering such questions will help you compose an outstanding résumé. Why? Because they point beyond "job title" and "dates of employment" to the Big Three: *skills*, *knowledge*, and *traits*. Every outstanding résumé incorporates life experiences that highlight all three.

Look Beyond Work

Society wrongly teaches us that life consists of two distinct kinds of activities—work and play. As a result, when we compose a résumé we tend to consider only work, especially paid employment. But is paid employment the only real work? Not a chance! In one sense, everything we do is work, regardless of compensation. But because of our truncated view of work, we rarely look beyond our paid employment for those life experiences that demonstrate work-related but not necessarily job-used skills, knowledge, and traits. Doing the things we love often teaches us more than we realize. We learn by doing. Before we know it, we're informed and skilled.

While working at various jobs during the day, my coauthor, Bethany Kim, spent evenings during the first three years after college collecting and cataloguing her own library of used children's books. She did it because she enjoyed the relaxing process. But at the same time she learned about budgeting, making business contacts, using spreadsheets, and building her own organizational framework—not to mention accruing a vast knowledge of authors and literature. What started as a personal passion became a great learning experience that eventually led to her writing her own books. You've undoubtedly had similar experiences in your life, experiences that have involved doing things about which you became passionate, whether or not you were paid to do them. What are they? What did you learn from those experiences?

Your passions are good places to begin describing yourself for a résumé, as long as you fine-tune your "answers" for each position or organization. Life is more than work. It's about people and passions. So are great résumés.

You can't predict all of the things you'll need to know or do in your career. Job descriptions are never final, especially advertised ones. That's why the best résumés reflect the range of your strengths—the "whole you"—including what you learned from non-work experiences that might transfer to paid work and eventually blossom into a career.

For instance, the following skills, knowledge, and traits are important for teaching:

■ "Performing" before an audience (keeping the students interested and motivated)

■ Preparing well but being flexible (sometimes the best teaching occurs when students ask unexpected questions or bring up their own examples)

■ Putting yourself in someone else's shoes (taking the point of view of a student, parent, or textbook)

■ Having fun and helping others enjoy learning (good learning is enjoyable, just as our pleasurable experiences almost always instruct while entertaining)

Dr. Q's tip

Your résumé should persuade by highlighting concretely what you've learned and what you can contribute to an organization as a result of your life experiences.

If you were writing a résumé for a teaching job, you'd probably want to include experiences that documented your most fitting skills, knowledge, and traits. Like other organizations, most schools admire employee loyalty. While working part time in a neighborhood pharmacy, I learned such loyalty—to the family that owned the drugstore and to the customers, such as the needy shut-ins to whom I delivered prescriptions. I also learned patience, respect, and openness to others' ideas. I learned to enjoy customers' sometimes offbeat senses of humor, as well as how to joke with them in friendly and yet appropriate ways. I gained confidence in awkward situations, such as responding to a customer's whispered request for condoms, which back then were kept behind the counter as an "adult" product. I came to appreciate the pharmacy owner's musical tastes by listening to the folk tunes and jazz solos

Dr. Q's tip

> Normally a late-college or post-college résumé should not include high school or earlier experiences. For those who attended high school recently, exceptions could include impressive honors or activities continued into college, like studying music for ten years (a good sign of your self-motivation and perseverance, if not musical talent).

he played all day long. These traits, as well as the skills and knowledge I acquired, served me well in later years as I became a consultant, teacher, mentor, and public speaker.

So even though you can't know for certain what you'll end up doing in the next five or ten years, you can examine your past work in order to document what you have learned about yourself that might help you serve others. Your own learned abilities represent the "life" you can offer to potential employers on your résumé.

In fact, the United States is one of only a few countries that uses the word *résumé*. Nearly everywhere else a résumé is called a *curriculum vitae* (pronounced "vee'-tay"), which is Latin for the "course of one's life." Some people call it a "CV" or just a "vita" (vee'-tuh).

Your résumé should reflect the career-relevant things you've learned at work *and* at play. It should document your self-knowledge, not just the jobs and positions you've held. What have you learned from your past work, even from your part-time, seemingly menial labor? From your life? You'll need to list and substantiate with examples the skills, knowledge, and traits you've already discovered in your life.

Expert Advice

> A résumé "is a written exaggeration of only the good things a person has done in the past, as well as a wish list of the qualities a person would like to have."
>
> Bo Bennett, *Year to Success*

As you'll see, life experience usually includes formal and informal education, paid employment, and other activities. It can even include volunteering and hobbies, significant travel, and cross-cultural experience.

Résumé Excerpt

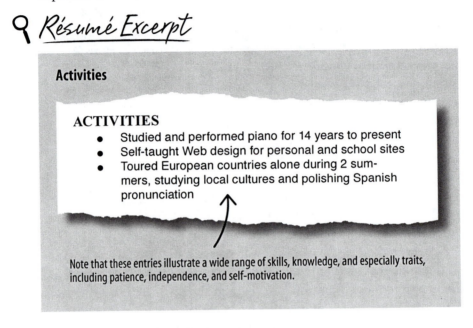

Activities

ACTIVITIES
- Studied and performed piano for 14 years to present
- Self-taught Web design for personal and school sites
- Toured European countries alone during 2 summers, studying local cultures and polishing Spanish pronunciation

Note that these entries illustrate a wide range of skills, knowledge, and especially traits, including patience, independence, and self-motivation.

Conclusion

When my résumé-writing workshop attendees started chattering about the phone numbers and e-mail addresses they had recently circulated on résumés, they were asking the same good questions that every career seeker should ask: questions about who we are and how we should use résumés to persuade potential employers to offer us an interview tomorrow, a month from now, or even later on when another opportunity opens up. As soon as one falls into the trap of thinking about a résumé as a list of former jobs, he or she is career-searching with a huge disadvantage. Human beings are whole people, not just paid workers. Our entire lives teach us how to serve others. So the best résumés—the interview-generating résumés—persuade potential employers of the range of job-related skills, knowledge, and traits we bring to our work.

In this sense, we're all wondering what we'll "be" when we grow up. Work is *part* of that growth process. Life *is* the growing. Specific occupations and entire careers will come and go along with economic shifts. Yet we'll still be learning how to use our potential in new, personally satisfying careers. Writing a résumé is an opportunity to explore afresh who we are and how and in what areas we can serve others.

What to Do Now

By now you recognize that an interview-generating résumé needs to capture your career potential, based on your life experiences. An effective résumé isn't merely a list of your job experiences. You've written a solid header with your name and numbers (gotta start somewhere!). Now take a few minutes to list at least ten of your most satisfying life experiences—making certain to look beyond paid positions. Explore and include any enjoyable and fulfilling volunteering, projects, travel, paid work, summer activities, hobbies, relationships, education, and so on—all of the stuff you're glad you had a chance to do. Use appendix A. This list will help you get your interview-generating résumé off the ground.

If you've already submitted weaker résumés, move ahead regardless.

Fortunately, many organizations don't retain older résumés. Moreover, you can always reapply at those organizations that most interest you. Just make sure you never get your name and number wrong.

Highlight Your Life Experiences

In this chapter you'll learn:

How to use résumés

How to develop a Masterlist of life experiences

How to expand your life experiences

In the midst of a very tight job market, one of my students asked me about getting a paid summer internship in radio. I didn't want to encourage him too much because it was already late in the spring, and very few stations still had open internships. Moreover, hardly any stations paid their interns. Nevertheless, I told the student that if he compiled his life experiences into a Masterlist of the items most closely related to radio broadcasting, I would help him compose a solid résumé and an accompanying cover letter. "Chances are slim, but one never knows," I thought to myself.

He came to my house on the following Saturday with a pretty good résumé and some great cover-letter material. We hammered out a final draft of each one. Then he sent the materials to radio stations around the state. We waited. I didn't expect many responses. So when my wife told me about a week later that I had received a phone call from a major radio station, I didn't connect the dots. I thought it was a station calling to interview me about a breaking news story, since I regularly receive interview requests. The call went something like this:

"Hello?"

"Dr. Schultze?"

"Yes."

"I'm Tim Barger, GM (general manager) of XYZ radio. I've got a résumé here from a student who lists you as a reference. Do you know Jim Smith?"

"Yes, I do."

"Well, are his résumé and cover letter accurate?"

"What do you mean?"

"I mean I don't think any college kid could be this good on paper."

"Well, if he sent you the same résumé I saw, I can verify that Jim is what he says."

"Really. Well, I'll tell you what. You send him over on Monday afternoon and I'll interview him personally. I'm a bit skeptical, but send him over."

"Thanks very much, Mr. Barger. I'll let him know right away."

We exchanged good-byes and I quickly called Jim to let him know what had happened. Jim showed up at the station on Monday, interviewed with the GM, and landed a paid internship for the summer. A year later he was hired full-time by the same station. Eventually I received a letter from Mr. Barger, asking whether I had any more students to send his way. I did. He hired more of them, first as paid interns and later on as full-time employees.

Here's the secret: Jim was not an outstanding student, but he had drive, desire, and a terrific personality. And he was willing to promote himself honestly on a résumé. He couldn't push radio-specific skills, because he lacked such experience. Instead, he emphasized his *related* skills, knowledge, and traits. He did so by creating a dynamite Master-list of life experiences and projects *based on the language used in the classified ads he'd read in broadcasting trade magazines.* Jim's résumé and cover letter caught the attention of one station's general manager, landed him an interview, and actually convinced the station to create a low-paying but experience-rich internship just for him. Ironically, he heard nothing back from any other station. It took just one station to launch his dream of working in broadcasting, and he's still in the field, thriving in a larger city.

This chapter first explains how résumés work in various situations beyond cold job applications, where applicants are merely responding to a position announcement or classified want ad. Next, the chapter builds on your work at the end of chapter 2 by showing you how to create an extensive Masterlist of past experiences so that you can accurately assess your skills, knowledge, and traits. That's exactly what Jim did with his radio résumé.

Use Great Résumés

An impressive résumé will help you get job interviews. It's important to remember that the purpose of a résumé is usually to get you in the door to meet people and sell yourself to an organization. But there are many ways to use résumés to generate interviews. There are also ways that employers use résumés to decide on and conduct interviews.

Networking

You're out for dinner with friends. A friend of a friend mentions that she's looking for an intern or a new employee. Your ears perk up. What should you say or do?

If you don't have a solid résumé, probably not too much. You'll ask a couple of questions and maybe exchange phone numbers—if you're lucky. Writing your name on a napkin won't make a great impression. You need a more professional calling card.

If you've got a great résumé that's ready to tweak and send out via fax, e-mail, or surface mail, you're in business. Your prep has paid off. Just tweak it for the specific organization, write an accompanying cover letter, and you're all set.

Here's the bottom line: Even if you've already got a job, always be ready to send out a polished résumé, because you never know who you're going to meet and who's going to request one. When somebody says to you, "Send me your résumé," you need to be prepared. A punctual reply is a great way of making a statement about one of the most important career traits: prompt-

Expert Advice 📖

Think Purpose

"When you prepare a résumé, always ask this penetrating question: 'What am I going to use this for?' The answer to that question will provide you with a 'road map' of what to include on your résumé."

Professor Jay Christensen, California State University at Northridge, quoted in *Ascribe Business & Economics News Service*

Dr. Q's tip

Improve your résumé by having a few friends ask you questions about the material on it. If their questions suggest that your résumé isn't very clear or convincing, rewrite it.

ness. You don't need to be in the market for a new position to begin networking with other people. After all, even if you have a job, you could be laid off tomorrow.

More and more employers are refraining from running want ads, especially for entry-level jobs. Instead, they first post positions internally. Then they try to hire by word of mouth, as needed. This way they don't have to deal with dozens or even hundreds of résumés for each position. Also, when they use the word-of-mouth method, an employee already knows the candidate; the applicant has at least one reference who can vouch for him or her, even before submitting a résumé. This way employers can often find three or four people to interview, based on résumés generated by trustworthy colleagues.

Job Interviewing

I was hunting for a part-time campus job that would teach me some marketable skills. I was fed up with brainless labor, especially the student cafeteria job where I stirred huge pots of soggy vegetables for two hours every evening. After a couple of months of that labor, my head looked—and felt—like an overcooked brussels sprout.

When somebody told me about a new opening in the university's audiovisual department, I ran over there, met the department manager, filled out an application, and scheduled an interview. I was excited. I couldn't believe that someone might actually pay me for taking photographs and making slides for professors.

"One more thing," the department manager requested before I left, "please bring along a résumé when you come back for the interview." A résumé? Huh? Besides selling condoms at the drug store and basting my body in veggie steam, what had I ever done? I was intimidated. Worried. Embarrassed. I didn't have a real résumé. I didn't even know what a "real" résumé was.

I cobbled together a list of previous part-time jobs, along with some related hobbies, including brief information about my own electronics equipment. Always a techno geek, I enjoy fixing everything from crashed computers to fried lamps, from wireless networks to satellite antennas. Much later in my life, when my adult son was home for the holidays, we bonded by fixing the motors that operate two windows in my rusted old VW.

Since the AV manager was busy and knew little about me, when I returned for the interview he simply asked me impromptu questions about the jobs and personal interests listed on my résumé. Fortunately, composing the résumé had prepped me for the interview, even though I blew the answers to some of the questions. My strengths? Hey, I work hard. I don't cheat the time clock. I get to work on time. Ironically, he was more impressed by my interest in electronics than by my actual jobs and self-reported strengths. We chatted about audio amplifiers, and he hired me on the spot. As it turned out, I would have to work with quite a bit of technology at the job. He was a techno geek, too. We could talk shop and learn from each other. Done deal.

Although it isn't *all* you need to do to prepare for an interview, writing a life-experience résumé is a useful step toward shaping your interviewer's questions. Sure, some interviewers use standard questions ("Where do you see yourself in five years?"), but this was a lowly campus job, not an executive-training track. I didn't expect questions about my résumé. I was naive. Often the résumé and cover letter are all the employers will know about you. That's why many employers use résumés for interviewing. A résumé functions as a script for the interview.

Winning Awards

You might unexpectedly need a great résumé for awards, scholarships, and better positions where you already work. Getting nominated for a special award or recognition is great, but the initial inquiry usually arrives unannounced: "So and so says you would be a good candidate

Expert Advice 📖

Write Your Résumé to Generate Interviews

"'The purpose of a résumé is to land you an interview.' Enough said."

Alexandra Levit, career columnist for the *Wall Street Journal* and author of *They Don't Teach Corporate in College* for the Up-and-Comer Award. Please send us a résumé so we can consider your qualifications." At that point, it's probably too late to start thinking about writing a résumé from scratch. You'll only have time to submit a slightly updated version of one you already have on hand.

Also, you might run across an advertised award you think you've got a shot at winning. My artsy older brother submitted a cover letter, a résumé, and some sculpture photos for a civic arts award. He surprised all of us by getting it—along with a substantial check and his photo in the paper. He had an award to put on his résumé, not to mention cash in his pocket.

Many nonprofit organizations, from local civic groups to religious organizations, offer awards. So do companies and governments. Colleges and universities offer special recognitions or at least award scholarships.

Climbing the Ladder

Or suppose you currently have a paid or unpaid internship or a part-time job or are volunteering at an organization. What happens if a job opens up while you're interviewing, working, or volunteering?

When an organization decides to hire one of its freelancers or temporary workers, it often wants to see a complete résumé even if it doesn't require a cover letter. Community service can be an important factor on such résumés. By maintaining a list of your pro bono (free, without compensation) activities, you'll be able to document all of your efforts, not just your paid employment. Many businesses appreciate hardworking employees who also give back to their communities as good citizens. They often prefer employees who will help generate positive publicity within the community.

Informational Interviewing

One the hottest means of networking is informational interviewing. Instead of a potential employer interviewing you, you turn the tables and interview him or her. Not because the employer has an immediate job opening, but simply because you want to find out more about that line of work.

Informational interviewing rules are simple. First, you can ask just about any question except something too personal (e.g., "How much do you make?"). Second, you should never make a job pitch ("Do you have any openings I could apply for?"). Informational interviews are among the best ways to explore various professions and organizations. But if you're the one asking the questions, how can your interviewer find out more about you?

Easy. Show your interviewer your résumé and ask for feedback. ("What should I change?" "What seem to be my job-related strengths and weaknesses?") I require my students to conduct two informational interviews after they complete their résumés. The students usually receive helpful résumé-related feedback specific to careers and organizations. Remember never to violate the informal code of informational interviewing ethics by asking for a job. Just say, "Thank you very much for your excellent advice, including the résumé feedback. I'll improve my résumé based on your helpful suggestions."

Dr. Q's tip

Never go to an informational interview without extra copies of your polished résumé. First, you can seek professional feedback on your résumé. Second, you can leave behind a couple of copies just in case your interviewer decides to alert others, within or outside of the organization, about your availability. Just ask this individual at the end of the informational interview whether she or he would like a couple of extra copies. Graciously allow them to decline. If they do ask for copies, let them determine what to do with them. Don't make suggestions.

Coauthor Bethany Kim considered changing her career path from teaching to publishing. Along the way she landed a first interview with the public relations department at a book publishing house. When she got there, however, she realized it was going to be less a formal interview than a chance for the employer to get to know her better. As it turned out, Bethany was able to learn a lot about PR work, too, just by asking the interviewer some questions. The job didn't pan out, but Bethany was far better prepared for later interviews for similar positions. Also, the interview gave her enough self-confidence to seek informational interviews in publishing. She learned enough to compose a publishing-oriented version of a résumé.

Dr. Q's tip

Many college students don't realize that résumés and interviews work together in the job-search process. Great résumés both generate interviews and guide the interviewers.

Applying for Graduate School

A growing number of graduate programs ask applicants to submit a professional résumé. Why? Partly because they want to know what an applicant has been doing besides studying. They frequently seek well-rounded applicants with varied life experiences, such as travel or interesting hobbies that could demonstrate a skill or knowledge helpful in campus-related work. Often they're searching for potential graduate students whose experience suggests that they might be a good college teaching or research assistant for a professor. In

Résumé Excerpt

Experience for a Grad School Research Assistant

B.A., Communications, Houten College, Casper, WY (20XX)
- Conducted extensive research for term paper on future of Internet streaming of TV programming, searching research databases and conducting interviews with 4 local TV station managers

Note that this entry demonstrates that you have the knowledge and skill to conduct secondary and primary research, along with the traits of courage and initiative to conduct real-world interviews.

short, they might pay you to attend grad school! It happens all the time. Graduate students call it a "free ride."

Suppose you're applying for a graduate degree in business, marketing, or management. You could spend $45,000 or more a year for grad school—and it might all be worth it in the end. With a solid résumé, though, you might discover that you don't have to pay the salaries of academic administrators. Why? Because you have some practical experience of value to the university—even if that experience isn't directly related to your major.

Here's a short list of experiences, some hobby-related, that have earned some of my students a free graduate education:

- Computer skills
- Desktop publishing experience
- Exceptional ability to search Internet research databases
- Experience creating user-friendly filing systems
- Familiarity with various bibliographic citation styles
- Experience organizing conferences and other events
- Knowledge of other languages and cultures

And this isn't an exhaustive list! Don't rule out the value of any experiences in which you may have developed unique skills. Besides, graduate school might be your best option for gaining additional skills and knowledge for launching a new career.

Create Your Masterlist

In order to develop résumés for any of these purposes, you'll need to expand the list of life experiences you started composing at the end of chapter 1. As you add new items and expand existing ones, keep in mind the various purposes for résumés. This will help you develop a Masterlist of life experiences from which you can select appropriate items for each new résumé aimed at a specific opportunity.

Dr. Q's tip

The key to creating great résumés is developing a Masterlist of your relevant life experiences for different jobs and purposes.

A Masterlist has three basic elements (see appendix a):

1. A chronological **list** of some of your relevant life experiences
2. A brief **analysis** of each of the experiences, according to what it demonstrates about your skills, knowledge, and traits
3. A concluding **summary** of your overall skills, knowledge, and traits

Positive experiences are usually more important than negative ones—unless you were able to transform a lousy experience into a good one. If, for example, your internship was challenging due to lack of employee communication at the organization where you worked, you probably learned a lot anyway. Did you independently develop a project? Did you come to recognize the value of teamwork? These might be important skills and knowledge you gleaned from a bad situation. If so, they deserve to be included on your Masterlist in spite of the downsides of the disappointing internship.

Negative experiences are opportunities for learning from your own and others' mistakes. This practical learning is one of the most important traits to highlight on a résumé. Even particularly disheartening work experiences can benefit you in terms of your next Masterlist update. Chances are they'll enable you to more accurately identify both your strengths and your weaknesses. If you were let go on the basis of poor organizational skills and inadequate follow-through, you're not so likely to allow those kinds of insufficiencies to affect your work in your next job. Besides, you'll probably have to include the episode on subsequent résumés (unless you were on the job for only a couple of days and you and your employer agreed it was a bad

Dr. Q's tip

Regularly update your Masterlist on your computer and print backup copies. Use appendix A to create your word-processing form for Masterlist entries, or visit the book website* to download a ready-to-go form.

Never delete items from your Masterlist, even if you don't use them in a current résumé. They might come in handy for later job or career changes. And reviewing your Masterlist is a great way to prepare for interviews. The Masterlist gives you plenty of examples and illustrations so you can offer concrete answers to interview questions.

*resumes4collegestudents.com

fit). When asked about a resignation or layoff in later interviews, you'll be better prepared to explain what you learned from the stressful event.

We've all had challenging work experiences. Unless we were blameless, we need to be able to discuss such experiences with potential employers. Rarely is it a good idea to try to hide a difficult work experience. Many interviewers will inquire about one- or two-year "gaps" in résumés anyway. Personal difficulties such as divorces and medical issues need not be addressed in résumés, let alone during interviews. Former jobs are a different story. They're fair game.

♀ *Résumé Excerpt*

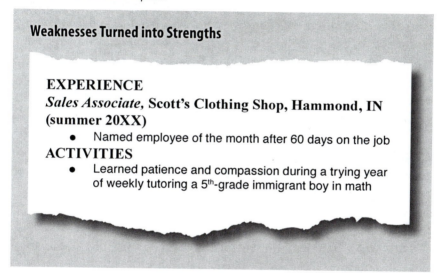

Weaknesses Turned into Strengths

EXPERIENCE
Sales Associate, **Scott's Clothing Shop, Hammond, IN (summer 20XX)**
- Named employee of the month after 60 days on the job

ACTIVITIES
- Learned patience and compassion during a trying year of weekly tutoring a 5th-grade immigrant boy in math

Some organizations go so far as to require applicants to fill out an official job application in addition to submitting a résumé. Normally the application requires a signature to attest to the fact that the application is "complete." A "complete" application must include all major, recent job experience. It's dishonest to skip such items. Do it at your own peril. And with your conscience open. Don't do anything along these lines that doesn't feel right and that you're unwilling to face with an employer if the issue comes up in spite of your attempt to keep it confidential.

🔆 *Dr. Q's tip*

Don't forget to include on your Masterlist—and probably on your résumé—technology skills, such as use of computers, software, and other digital devices in conjunction with hobbies, schooling, or volunteering. Technology skills are highly demanded in many careers.

Do include major negative experiences in your Masterlist, but don't dwell on them as you add more items to your list. Instead, add observations about how you dealt with those experiences at the time or subsequently. What was the positive result of your negative experience?

Generally speaking, you shouldn't include on a résumé anything that could be perceived as a negative comment about a former employee or a volunteer supervisor. Such negative comments suggest that you're blaming others for your own poor performance and that you might not yet be willing to accept your own weaknesses. Maybe even that you're vindictive and unforgiving. In an interview, you might have to say something negative about a former employer. In that case, be as kind and charitable as possible. But don't include *any* negative remarks on your résumé or in your cover letter.

Expand Your Experiences

Identifying meaningful life experiences can be frustrating until you get the hang of it. Here are some common categories to help you flesh out your Masterlist:

- **Major hobbies**—individual and team sports, other outdoor activities, collecting, and entertainment

- **Paid employment**—full-time and part-time jobs, including minimum-wage positions, summer work, short-term projects, temp agency fill-ins, and your own mini business selling goods or services to friends, family, or neighbors

- **Volunteer activities**—helping at civic, religious, political, and other institutions, including leading tours, hosting events, writing or speaking, managing files, organizing people, responding to inquiries, or interacting with the public

- **Travel**—family vacations, personal trips, college-related sports trips or performance tours, treks on behalf of employers and volunteer groups

- **Cultural experiences**—visits to other countries, college-sponsored tours or semester-abroad programs, spring break volunteer experiences in urban or rural areas, time spent living in different ethnic or racial areas, participation in exchange programs, and volunteer or paid jobs requiring interaction with a wide range of people

- **Formal learning**—skills and knowledge gained from college and university courses, workshops, conferences, internships, educational summer camps, research and writing projects, co-op programs, group presentations, assisting professors or other college staff, or employee training programs occurring on or off campus

- **Informal learning**—skills and knowledge achieved from your personal study and reflection, such as from reading books and magazines, searching online materials, viewing documentary or other educational films and videos, and teaching yourself computer hardware and software, including proprietary software written for and used by only one organization

- **Organizational participation**—any active memberships or leadership activities and responsibilities in social, religious, civic, hobby, school, political, and other organizations

- **Family circumstances**—helping to raise siblings, earning family support in addition to personal income, working extensively while attending school, caring for

Dr. Q's tip

Recall life experiences by picturing where you worked, volunteered, and pursued hobbies. We remember best when we rely on visual cues. If you have photos, use them to refresh your memories of people, places, and tasks.

-`Ọ`- Dr. Q's tip

If you're currently in college or have recently (within the last two years) attended college (even if you didn't graduate), review your academic transcript, previous course syllabi, and available college papers to recall special papers, projects, presentations, and courses worth including on your Masterlist.

Don't limit your list to items that seem immediately applicable to your career choice. You might change your career goals. You might discover later that a given career requires different skills, knowledge, and traits than what you had assumed. At this stage, be comprehensive.

parents or grandparents, or taking on any other family-related responsibilities

■ **Personal honors**—things that others have said you do well, perhaps resulting in awards, honors, recognitions, admissions to groups or programs, honorary memberships, affirming letters or e-mails, or media coverage

Spend an hour reviewing these categories and listing whatever comes to mind in each one—don't worry about eliminating any experiences at this point. Be open to considering experiences other than those listed above, even those that don't seem to fit into any of the categories or don't obviously lend themselves to inclusion on a résumé. These might prove to be helpful later on for particular résumés or interviews.

Sample Masterlist Excerpts

■ Spent three weeks last summer traveling in Mexico, learning the transportation systems, getting to know the locals, visiting museums, improving my conversational Spanish, becoming more independent, and getting acquainted with another culture

■ Taught 4th-grade Sunday school during my freshman and sophomore years, learning patience and the value of preparation

■ Served as a summer lifeguard at a country club, where I figured out how to work with demanding supervisors and befriended troubled kids, some of whom still e-mail me for advice.

One or more of these items could be developed for and used on a specific résumé for a particular internship, job, or even graduate school—such as, for example, in a social work program.

Masterlist Entries

LIFE EXPERIENCE:	
WHAT, WHEN AND WHY	Describe here *what* you did, *when* you did it, and *why* you did it.
SKILLS	Describe here what you learned to *do*.
KNOWLEDGE	Describe here what you learned *about*.
TRAITS	Describe here what you learned about *yourself*.

Develop Your Entries

The next step is to spend an hour reviewing and developing the items on your Masterlist. The basic question you want to ask yourself is what your life experience has taught you about the Big Three—your skills, knowledge, and traits. Chances are that you'll initially find this activity a bit challenging. Most of us are so busy with day-to-day tasks that we don't take the time to assess the value of our life experiences.

Masterlist Example

LIFE EXPERIENCE:	Arts and Crafts Director, Camp Run-A-Muk
WHAT, WHEN, AND WHY	During the summer of 20— I was Arts and Crafts Director at Camp Run-A-Muk in Muskegon, WV. I planned arts and crafts activities for kids ages 7-14, organized the crafts building, budgeted and ordered materials, and helped with evening activities as needed.
SKILLS	Budget materials, plan crafts, entertain kids, change plans at the last minute, organize my day.
KNOWLEDGE	Appropriate crafts for kids ages 7-14, different crafts catalogs, how to order materials, using few materials to do a lot
TRAITS	Hard working, creative, organized, thrifty, prompt, flexible, impatient with some kids.

You might want to use a separate page for each entry in your Masterlist. In any case, organize entries in a chart like the one above. (Also see appendix A.)

Soon you'll discover that a few of your life experiences are especially important because they say the most about your skills, knowledge, and traits. More than likely, these are the items you'll want to expand on your Masterlist. If you discover some negative traits (e.g., impatience or disorganization), include them on your Masterlist. Later on you'll have an opportunity to determine whether you have addressed (or should address) such weaknesses prior to finalizing your résumé and eventually preparing for interviews. One of the standard interview questions is what you perceive as your weaknesses and what you've been doing to address those deficits.

Use the subcategories below to help you flesh out specific skills, knowledge, and traits.

Identify Your Skills

Knowing your skills is critically important for writing a résumé. But there are various categories of skills to consider. Use the categories below to identify the types of skills you have so that you can be sure to address them concretely in your résumé.

Dr. Q's tip

Social, personal, and *learning* skills often overlap in the same life experiences. Since these are not entirely separate categories, don't worry about determining exactly where to list one of your skills. Just use the three categories to help you identify and record them. Later on you can move the items to different categories or even list them in multiple categories. Just make sure to identify some skills for each of the three categories. All work requires social, personal, and learning skills.

1. **Social** skills—skills that help you interact with others (e.g., listening, serving, encouraging, organizing groups, and leading people)
2. **Personal** skills—skills that help you accomplish things on your own (e.g., organizing information, repairing things, journaling, and planning)
3. **Learning** skills—skills that help you gain knowledge and acquire social and personal skills (e.g., studying, writing, training, listening, memorizing, solving problems, and practicing)

Suppose that while working as a restaurant host or server you learned social skills, such as how to satisfy difficult customers, how to get along well with coworkers, and how to interact in a friendly way with managers who were sometimes stressed out or overly demanding. You might even have realized that you are better at these skills than

📖 *Expert Advice*

Demonstrate Essential Life Skills

"While your level of education is important on a résumé, some life skills might be even more important in the eyes of employers: *problem solving, communication, technology,* and *time management.*"

Diane Nelson Bryen, et. al., "So You Want to Work? What Employers Say about Job Skills, Recruitment and Hiring Employees Who Rely on AAC," *Augmentative and Alternative Communication*

many of the other employees. Such skills suggest that you have the ability to establish healthy and productive work relationships, even with difficult colleagues.

Maybe you helped organize an event for a college, religious, or social organization. Apart from interacting with others in the planning group, you personally wrote a brief event plan, created a budget, and found a location for the event. In other words, you called upon various individual and *learning* skills, such as writing, budgeting, and scheduling. Suppose the planning group didn't work well together. Members argued about issues or procedures. You stepped in to help members get along by reducing their conflicts through good humor or practical advice. Clearly you have some important *social* skills, such as the ability to lead others and to help resolve interpersonal conflicts.

Perhaps you agreed to try your hand at publicizing the event, even though you had never done such work before. On your own, you found out what needed to be done in order to effectively promote the event, and you followed through on your findings. Chances are you relied upon critically important *learning* and *social* skills—interviewing knowledgeable persons, conducting online research about how to plan such an event, and tracking down the basics of budgeting.

After completing your Masterlist, look it over one more time to ensure that the skills section is fleshed out. Think about *why* you did or didn't enjoy using particular skills. Even if you can do something well you might not enjoy it enough to continue doing it for the rest of your life. Make appropriate personal notes to yourself. No one needs to see your Masterlist except you. Think of your Masterlist as a personal journal, not a public résumé. You don't need to show anyone your personal journal, so don't worry about privacy.

For example, suppose your Masterlist suggests that you enjoy and are talented in the area of travel. Ask yourself what you have most enjoyed about the travel experience. Did you like meeting people and forming new friendships? Did you take pleasure in planning the trips, scheduling daily activities, and following through on your arrangements? Did you most appreciate what you learned about other places and cultures? Again, these are basically social, personal, and learning skills, respectively.

Assess Your Knowledge

Regardless of your specific past and current paid work experience, you're on a lifelong adventure, learning about people, places, issues, experiences, professions, hobbies, and more. So it's critically important for you to examine your life experiences in terms of your areas of knowledge, even if some of your specific knowledge doesn't seem relevant to a particular job. You never know which seemingly unrelated area of knowledge will appeal to an employer. Also, the kinds of work that interest you will likely change over time; past experience could have future value as you change jobs, careers, or professions.

Don't limit your list to immediately practical or "applied" knowledge. Think about what you know, even if you don't foresee how you might apply that knowledge to a particular job or task. All knowledge has practical value, even if you can't figure out on your own where or how to make it marketable.

There are three basic categories of knowledge:

1. **People** knowledge—knowledge of personalities, cultures, lifestyles, societies, ethnic groups, and religions

2. **Organizational** knowledge—knowledge of how types of organizations function, including businesses, nonprofits, families, online groups, clubs, governments, and schools

3. **Topical** knowledge—knowledge of particular subjects, such as entertainment (music, TV shows, and movies), nature (from gardening and landscaping to weather), technology (software and hardware), sports, and hobbies

℞ *Résumé Excerpt*

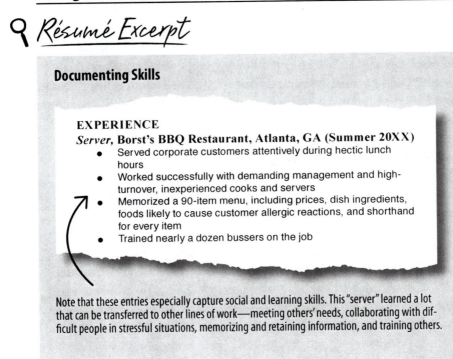

Documenting Skills

EXPERIENCE
Server, **Borst's BBQ Restaurant, Atlanta, GA (Summer 20XX)**
- Served corporate customers attentively during hectic lunch hours
- Worked successfully with demanding management and high-turnover, inexperienced cooks and servers
- Memorized a 90-item menu, including prices, dish ingredients, foods likely to cause customer allergic reactions, and shorthand for every item
- Trained nearly a dozen bussers on the job

Note that these entries especially capture social and learning skills. This "server" learned a lot that can be transferred to other lines of work—meeting others' needs, collaborating with difficult people in stressful situations, memorizing and retaining information, and training others.

As you develop the knowledge category in your Masterlist, try to think outside professional boxes. Bear in mind that your Masterlist is a tool for your personal preparation. You can't predict when knowledge of particular people, organizations, and topics will serve you well—hobbies included. One of the biggest mistakes college students make is assuming that they know in advance precisely what's needed for a particular career. College courses don't adequately prepare you for everything you'll need to know on the job. They don't even cover all of the necessary knowledge. Academic textbooks are like software owners' manuals; they never cover everything a user needs to know, and even when they do explain the action steps for accomplishing something, it's not always easy to follow through.

One of my students possessed an astounding degree of knowledge of classical and contemporary Hollywood movies. Nearly every night she watched an entire film, including the credits. She perused large movie guidebooks in the same way some people read novels or sports news. She could easily identify actors and actresses by their photographs, recite the films in which they had appeared, and assess the quality of their performances. Her knowledge and memory of films amazed me.

Yet she was clueless about the value of her extensive movie knowledge for her résumé and in the job market. Eventually I directed her to the field of talent casting. Her movie-watching, actor-studying hobby became a marketable asset in commercial video production when she secured a position casting local and regional actors. Local producers gave her role/character descriptions based upon producers' knowledge of Hollywood performers: "I need a Jim Carrey-like goofball who is facially expressive, vocally silly, and wildly uninhibited to do a commercial for a regional water park." Casting a role like that was easy for her. Her knowledge and passion for movies had become a valuable commodity. Yet she didn't recognize this until I pointed it out to her. She had assumed that her developing movie knowledge would never go beyond a hobby. How wrong she was.

Or suppose you're a nerd of sorts. You've seen every episode of *Stargate SG-1*. You love playing Scrabble. You collect cookbooks. You write fan fiction online. Given all of these activities, what are your areas of knowledge? Science fiction? Language? Cooking? Used book buying? Take the time to examine your unique Masterlist to see what you can learn about yourself. This insight will help you later on to compose résumés for particular positions. Your past is a gateway to your future. So map out your past before charging ahead.

Know Your Personal Traits

Along with identifying your skills and knowledge, you need to recognize your traits. Your traits are *the ways you tend to behave*—the *style* of your work and play rather than its substance. For instance, how do you interact with coworkers? How would your former coworkers or classmates describe you? What are you like as a human being? If you're not sure, it's time to find out so you can shore up your strengths and address apparent weaknesses on your résumé.

Human traits can change over time, even though they partly reflect our inherited personalities. A shy person can learn to become more outgoing. A perfectionist can become less fussy. A mild-mannered person can learn to be a bit more assertive when appropriate. But our basic tendencies aren't easy to change. We are who we are. So it's best to write a résumé that accurately captures your basic traits. Your personal goals should be to build upon your strengths and minimize your weaknesses, in work as in life. In addition, you'll do best in a career that complements your best traits.

Identifying your seemingly negative traits can help you in determining your positive qualities. For example, disorganized people tend to be creative. They generate a lot of great ideas, even if they have trouble completing projects based upon their ideas. Good writers are often introverts, uncomfortable with public speaking. Somehow, being introverted seems to help them use solitude to collect their thoughts, express their ideas, and then polish their prose. I know many introverted scientists who love working solo in the lab, day after day. I would go stir crazy. When I'm completing something on deadline, however, I thrive on peace and quiet. I don't even want music in the background. I've chased away noisy crows from our back yard; their random screechy squawks were driving me loony. All it took was the discharge of my son's BB rifle to scare them off for the rest of the day.

There are worthwhile personality assessment tools, such as the Myers-Briggs. I encourage you to take them. They can help you discover your traits. Most colleges offer these assessments free of charge, and some organizations require all employees to take them. Many can be completed online. They will help you learn more about yourself. Besides, it's fun to swap results with friends and family. You'll probably discover why you gravitate to some people more than to others.

For the immediate purpose of writing a solid résumé, however, you can simplify trait categories. A persuasive résumé should address at least two key trait categories: *motivation* and *relationships*. So examine your Masterlist in terms of these two categories:

Motivation—*tangible or intangible*

What motivates you? Financial or other tangible benefits, such as awards and trophies? Praise from customers, clients, bosses, or friends? Or less tangible factors, such as a personal sense of pleasure or accomplishment? As you examine your Masterlist, you should begin to identify patterns of tangible or intangible motivation, unless you happen to be the kind of person who is motivated equally by both. Do you prefer or find yourself satisfied with intangible recognition for a job well done? For example, do you enjoy just knowing that you've helped others? I do quite a bit of freelance work for others—mentoring, coaching, editing, conducting focus groups, and giving interviews—partly because I enjoy the work and like serving people. Except for the purposes of paying the bills and saving modestly for retirement, I don't personally require a salary or wages. I would like to learn more in order to give more to worthy causes; serving others motivates me more than does personal compensation.

Sometimes students tell me that money motivates them but that they wouldn't want potential employers to know that. Well, there are a couple of problems with this view. First, money can motivate without becoming one's primary motivation. How we rank our desires in life is very important. Loving money doesn't have to be the highest priority in life. Nor is it exactly the same as desiring to live comfortably. Loving friends and family should be a higher desire than loving paychecks. We all need to prioritize our life desires in tune with our personal motivations.

Second, financial rewards are important in many careers. Salespeople can serve their customers well, even as they seek to increase sales. Most entrepreneurs take risks partly to be able to enjoy the fruit of their invested time, energy, and financial support. It isn't unusual for any organization to evaluate job applicants partly on the basis of whether the prospective employees really want to succeed. "Where do you see yourself in five years?" is a common interview question. Passion and drive can be excellent traits. So it's not surprising that financial incentives do boost passion and drive for some career seekers.

Relationship—*group or solo style*

How do you prefer working? Do you like meetings and group projects? Do you get antsy if you're alone and on your own all day? Are you more introverted than extroverted? Do you prefer working solo, without distractions, free to focus on the task before you?

One of the things I really enjoy about college-level teaching is interacting with students, both in and out of the classroom. The relationships motivate me to teach and mentor well. I don't enjoy sitting alone in my office, grading exams or papers. Sometimes I'm able to complete my grading by going to a café, buying a cup of coffee and a muffin, and sitting there in a quiet corner for two hours or more with a red pen and a stack of papers. Just being out somewhere with other people around helps me to complete the task—as long as the place isn't excessively noisy.

Originally I was hoping to become an engineer because I enjoy learning about electronics. When I discovered years ago that much engineering work is a solo activity, however, I looked for a different college major. The first course I took on human communication hooked me. I loved talking about talking! Three decades later I still love communicating about communication. Seeing students get excited about communication really motivates me. My own résumé lists a lot of activities, particularly those that have to do with me communicating with others about communication. Fortunately, my college is willing to pay me to do what I enjoy.

Now you see why I'm interested in résumés as persuasive communication. But here's a secret: I wasn't always an outgoing, relationship-oriented person. Throughout high school I was a shy loner. I had just never learned social skills. Once I went away to college, I found that I had to work with others. To my own surprise, I liked it. I gradually discovered more surprises about myself. For one thing, I'm not as shy as I had once thought that I was. I've spoken to 15,000 people at a time. Obviously, I changed as I learned more about myself and gained self-confidence.

Conclusion

As you develop your Masterlist entries, think about what sets you apart from other potential candidates. Employers would like to see that you've gone beyond the standard duties of a particular job, volunteer activity, or hobby. Everybody who works in retail runs transactions and helps customers; there's nothing special about that work. So what did *you* do in retail that demonstrated your particular skills, knowledge, and traits? Did you win the title of employee of the month, set up a new filing system, or sell more products than any other employee in a given time period? Did you work hours no one else wanted to take—like Friday and Saturday evenings (flexibility)? Did you stay at the job longer than was typical (loyalty)?

Of course, you're not Superman or Superwoman, so you can't excel at everything. But incorporating your own trait-demonstrating accomplishments wherever possible will really make your résumé stand out. Don't lie. Don't hype. Be concrete. If you're honest, your Masterlist will help you not just with your résumé but with your eventual interviews as well. Think about yourself as an employee. Why would others want to work with you? What could you do for them, no matter how general or mundane? Focus on these kinds of experiences, and you'll get noticed. You'll land an interview, just like my former student who snagged a last-minute radio internship.

What to Do Now

Now is the time to complete the three-part chart (appendix A) for every significant item in your Masterlist. If the material you already included for an item strikes you as something you would be willing to talk about in a job interview, flesh out the wording for that item to highlight possible *skills*, *knowledge*, and *traits* that it reflects. Use the lists of skills, knowledge, and traits in this chapter to jog your memory. Visit www.resumes4collegestudents.com for downloadable forms.

Also be sure to complete the basic background information about *when*, *where*, and *why* you had each experience. Include the exact name and address of the place or organization. You'll be well on the way from college to a career-launching résumé and subsequent interviews.

Write for Your Audience

In this chapter you'll learn:

How to focus your résumé content for your audience
How to organize your résumé for your audience

While writing this book I distributed manuscript copies to human resources (HR) directors and career coaches for feedback. They offered many helpful suggestions, but their greatest contribution was pointing out the top reason résumés (and cover letters) so often fail to generate interviews: The résumés are not written for the specific organization and position. Too many résumés are weakly generic; they could be sent to practically any organization for a host of different positions. As one HR director put it, "Tell your readers to write their résumés for the company, not for themselves." That's great advice.

So I decided to dedicate an entire chapter to the topic of writing a résumé for a specific audience. This is a key, if not *the* key, to composing an interview-generating résumé. *Employers want to see in the résumé that you know something about the organization and about the open position.* Moreover, they expect you to relate your general experience to the type of work you'd be doing should you be hired for the position. Cover letters can help you connect your experience to the job, but they can't do it persuasively without a solid, audience-oriented résumé. In other words, avoid using the same résumé for every job application. Fine-tune each résumé, as well as each cover letter. Think in terms of what the organization wants to read, not in terms of what you want to write. Put yourself in the organization's "shoes."

A great résumé persuasively presents parts of your life story to a particular organization and for a specific career track. It does this by drawing the audience into your story as quickly as possible. Most employers are busy. They see a lot of résumés and speedily assess each one. The most effective way to engage a busy reader is to begin your résumé with a one-sentence summary that focuses his or her attention on how *you* can *serve them*—not merely on what you want *from them*.

Before you can write a great summary, however, you need to organize your relevant Masterlist entries for your résumé. Once you have a rough draft of your résumé, you can craft your summary. Your summary must encapsulate your life story, as expressed in your résumé. In other words, your résumé should concretely support your summary, so that there is no doubt to a reader that you are who you claim to be.

College students find it most helpful to organize their Masterlist items according to three résumé categories: *experience*, *education*, and *activities*. As you review your Masterlist entries, you'll be able to fill in these categories, creating a résumé that weaves together a convincing story about you. Along the way, you might also include an additional category or two highlighting your skills, knowledge, and traits for a specific audience (i.e., for a particular job or organization).

Know Your Audience

One key to writing a top-notch résumé is translating your life experiences for a specific purpose, such as for securing a particular internship, a specific job, or a special volunteer position. Don't even try cramming everything that's included on your Masterlist into your résumé. That's like taking bits and pieces from different songs and trying to write a beautiful new melody with them. It doesn't work. One résumé can't be all things to all employers, let alone for all careers. As one savvy employer put it to me, "The worst résumés are written by no one in particular for everyone in general." In other words, you need to know both yourself and your audience. Only then can you connect the dots between the two.

So go back through your Masterlist and select experiences that are probably most relevant to your audience. Your audience is simply the people who are going to be reading your résumé and assessing your fit for an interview for a particular position. The items you select should relate your skills, knowledge, and traits to the employer's needs and interests for the kind of position you hope to obtain.

Basic Résumé Categories:

Name
Contact Info
SUMMARY
EXPERIENCE
EDUCATION
ACTIVITIES

Don't get anxious about lacking qualifications for a first-career résumé. Nearly every career-seeking applicant lacks at least some qualifications. Anyone who is new to a particular line of work is by definition under-qualified. In fact, employers often prefer to hire a willing first-timer with the right skills over a more experienced applicant who will have to unlearn specific ways of doing things and then relearn how the new organization operates. In most cases your résumé doesn't need to demonstrate that you already have all the qualifications, but only that you have the related kinds of skills, knowledge, and traits that would make you a good fit and predict the likelihood of your success.

Many job descriptions for new-to-the-field positions even express the organization's willingness to consider candidates who are under-qualified but particularly promising. For instance, a description might say something like this: "Qualifications: 2–3 years marketing research *or similar experience*." What is "similar experience"? It means that you can demonstrate that you have the abilities that would prepare you to learn quickly what the new job requires. You might not know a lot about marketing, let alone about marketing particular goods and services. But you can think and act like a marketer and, in this case, a researcher. You're a curious person. You like to teach yourself about things. You enjoy discovering the "facts" behind things other people take for granted. In short, you don't make rash decisions; you do your homework (your *due diligence*) before making important decisions. You're a good fit even if not specifically qualified by on-the-job experience.

I've seen this repeatedly with my own college students. They apply for job after job in the field of their academic major, only to obtain the one job they apply for that isn't connected with their major! This phenomenon drove me crazy until I figured out what was going on. I learned from employers that when it comes to entry-level jobs, organizations often look for the right kind of person—the person with the most *fitting* skills and traits—rather than for people with a particular degree, specific job experiences, and particular professional knowledge.

But how can you be certain what a résumé reader is looking for? For instance, which basic skills, knowledge, and traits does a given employer really seek? What will grab the attention of someone sifting through a stack of résumés submitted for a specific position?

You can't determine this conclusively, especially since employers themselves don't always know in advance precisely what they're looking for. The HR staff and the employee-seeking department might not fully agree, either. Frequently they launch a search with the intent of hiring someone who has all of the experience stated in a job description. But when they start reviewing résumés they see other kinds of experience and knowledge that start them thinking: "Maybe we should consider John Doe because he's got experience with 'X' even though he lacks 'Y'." Sometimes the "quality of the person" and that individual's "career potential" become more significant than the applicant's specific job experience—especially for entry-level openings.

Nevertheless, you need to focus your résumé on the likely audience as best you can. Remember, a generic résumé written for everyone isn't likely to appeal to anyone in particular. Know who you are. Know what the job is likely to entail. Then connect the dots on your résumé and summarize the connections in your summary statement. This résumé-writing strategy might be the most important single lesson I've learned in 30 years of helping career seekers secure interviews and attain jobs. I call it "fit." You want your

Expert Advice

Know Thy Company as Thy Self

Make sure that "you research the companies as much as they research you."

Toby Freedman, *Career Opportunities in Biotechnology and Drug Development* résumé to fit the job and the organization. And you want the résumé readers to see you as a good fit.

Doing additional research about jobs and organizations can be time consuming, but it's critically important. You need to determine both what employers are looking for and what you have to offer. In the end, the extra "up front" time you put into building a fitting résumé will save you time later on by eliminating dozens of ineffective résumés. I urge you to invest the time at the beginning of the process. Nothing can be more demoralizing for career seekers than sending out dozens of resumes and receiving no call-backs for interviews. Why put yourself through that kind of unproductive and confidence-eroding experience?

There are fairly standard expectations for minimally accomplished people entering any career field or position. In every career, employers hold common assumptions about what they would like you to do (*skills*), know (*knowledge*), and be like (*traits*). Your résumé needs to relate your life experiences to that audience's common expectations—what *they* want, not merely what *you* want! You need to demonstrate the connections between things you *have* done and what a particular employer *needs* done.

How can you do this? The answer is one of the best-kept secrets about résumé writing. And it works—really works. The secret is this: Find out the specific language professionals in a given field use to describe the kinds of general skills and traits you possess. Then use *their* language on *your* résumé. Before you make the final decisions about which items from your Masterlist to include on a position-specific résumé, do one or more of the following:

■ Examine at least six classified ads for positions similar to the one you're applying for in order to determine which skills, knowledge, and traits are being sought. Use online search engines or, better yet, trade publications—magazines aimed at professionals by their field and listed by profession in *Ulrich's Periodicals Directory*, which is available in hard copy at most libraries and probably available online at your college with a student login.

- Speak with at least two people who have more than three years of experience in the field for which you're preparing a résumé. Ask friends and relatives for the names and contact information of persons in the field, or request an official informational interview with someone in your community whose name you obtain from general Internet searches or local news media. If you're a college student or alumnus, see whether your college placement office has an alumni networking database of graduates by field of work.

- Review at least two online articles about recent hiring practices in the field (use "Google News" or any of the business and news periodical research databases available at a library).

- Speak with at least two college instructors who themselves have recent experience in the field (they can probably direct you to sources with regard to the preceding two bullet points, as well).

If you'd really like to write a dynamite résumé, do all four of the above. Believe me, the effort will exponentially increase your chances of landing an interview. You'll also be much better prepared for interviews. You'll probably run across open positions along the way as well. So if you have time, do all four.

Once you've completed one or more of these steps, write a list of the key words and phrases you've discovered. For instance, here are some words and phrases in current *business-related* want ads, both in a local paper and on its website:

- responsible
- skillful
- excellent communication skills
- computer experience
- attention to details
- common sense
- desire to learn

- setting goals
- working independently
- self-starter

Here are some for a *retail management* job at a specialty shop:

- experienced managing staff
- inventory control
- ordering, marketing
- good attitude
- organized
- customer-service skills
- schedule flexibility

Here are a few for *health care* positions:

- flexibility
- excellent communication skills
- able to maintain strict confidentiality
- knowledge of Native American culture

Finally, here are some additional phrases from a range of ads for various positions:

- solid analytical skills
- due diligence and excellent follow-through skills
- ability to prioritize and multitask
- training staff
- upbeat and outgoing
- energetic
- ability to work with limited supervision
- above-average PC/Excel skills
- advanced computer skills
- ability to work within a team
- proven ability to manage multiple projects from cradle to grave (no kidding!)

Once you've compiled and written out the career-related, job-specific phrases, sort them out by skills, knowledge, and traits. Then put checks next to the ones that match the skills, knowledge, and traits from your Masterlist. You're going to compose your résumé and later your cover letter with these phrases in mind. They'll be the primary links between your general life experience and the specific responsibilities for a particular position in a specific organization for a distinct career. Note that your Masterlist provides the specific supporting examples from your life experience.

A word to the wise: Avoid the temptation to use these key phrases verbatim in your résumé if you can't support them with your actual experiences. Always use such key phrases honestly and appropriately in your résumé (especially in your summary statement, as I'll explain shortly). Résumés are not good places for idle boasting or for bending the truth. This is the most common ethical issue to consider.

Dr. Q's tip

Don't be concerned if your résumé categories don't exactly match those used in generic guides distributed by university career development offices. Also, don't fret about adding a category or two to the ones suggested. Feel free to fine-tune the precise names of my suggested categories, especially as you discover more about your career field. Résumé experts always acknowledge exceptions. The most important critics of your résumé are those working in the career field for which you drafted the résumé. They provide the most relevant, wisest advice about things like résumé length, wording, categories, and formatting.

Some employers may scan your résumé just for "key words." They might even scan it into a computer. If you include the right key words, borrowed from classified ads and the like, employers will be more inclined to give your résumé special attention. Of course, you'll still need to dedicate time to carefully preparing your whole résumé. Remember that your audience might not have a lot of time to review every incoming résumé; an assistant might conduct the initial review in order to flag the most fitting résumés for the boss or a search committee. In fact, I've seen people land interviews and even get positions because a résumé's key words demonstrated to employers that the applicant cared enough about the profession to do the research and then to document on their résumé their key word-related skills, knowledge, and traits. Employers saw the personal fit because the résumé writer made the fit too obvious to ignore.

Hopefully you now understand that résumé writing is not a one-time event. After you have completed and analyzed your Masterlist, the hard part is over. But each time you apply for a position you'll have to review both your Masterlist and your résumé to see whether you need to tweak the résumé for the audience. Moreover, if you're applying for positions in a field that you haven't yet researched for key words, you'll need to conduct a new search. The good news is that you'll get better and better at the process, and it will go more quickly as you elicit helpful feedback, gain additional practice, and boost your self-confidence. Once you employ the key words in your résumé and cover letter, you'll witness an immediate improvement in the number of interview requests. Just don't let the success make you lazy when you apply for jobs with different kinds of organizations and new types of positions.

Organize Your Content

My experience has demonstrated that there are three highly effective categories for organizing a college résumé: *experience*, *education*, and *activities*—normally in that order. You'll find additional categories in résumé-writing guides and in sample résumés distributed by career development professionals. Frankly, there are many fitting ways to organize résumés, especially for people at different life stages. This book focuses on current college students and recent graduates. These three categories have repeatedly proven to afford both the flexibility and the structure for a solid college and post-college résumé.

Resist the urge to create your own categories based on generic advice from self-appointed experts. When it comes to résumé-writing, everyone seems to feel as though they're an expert—even if they haven't written a résumé or reviewed

Dr. Q's tip

As you copy items from your Masterlist into the main categories on your résumé, avoid literary perfection; you're better off polishing the language later. Focus first on basic, audience-specific content, not literary style. Get the essentials down on paper before worrying about improving your prose. Others can help you copyedit the text, but *you* have to draft the basic material because you know your life better than anyone else does.

someone else's for a decade. These know-it-alls love doling out advice: You have to include references in your résumé; never, ever use a two-page résumé; if you were fired from your last job, just lie about it; always put your education first; never include hobbies on a résumé. These kinds of résumé-writing "rules" are like online urban legends that just never die. If only résumé writing were so "scientific"! What you really need in a résumé is *flexibility* within *structure*. The three résumé categories used in this book provide both. Below is a further description of what to include when you translate material from your Masterlist into relevant key words for your résumé. Always keep in mind the specific employer/audience. Don't write to make yourself feel good. Write to demonstrate that you've got what it takes for a particular field, fine-tuned to a specific position.

State Your Experience

When most employers, supervisors, and human resource personnel look at a résumé, they zero in on the person's experience. So most résumé writers understandably use categories such as "work experience" or "job experience."

The problem is that few college students have enough specific, "official" (i.e., paid) work experience to adequately develop such narrowly focused categories. So they list part-time employment and perhaps some full-time employment for seemingly unrelated jobs—the last few paid positions they've held, whether flipping burgers, parking cars, waiting on customers, retail clerking, or mowing lawns. To make matters worse, first-career seekers often fail to describe what they actually did in and learned from those jobs (the skills, knowledge, and traits they acquired). They just list the jobs, as though the jobs speak for themselves. The trouble is that job titles don't stand on their own, so you need to briefly explain the work you did at the job. What you learned.

Keep two things in mind: (1) that "experience" is more than just paid work,

📖 *Expert Advice*

Look Beyond Work

Normally you should include internships, volunteer work, and summer jobs on your résumé. "Just because you didn't get paid for something doesn't mean it doesn't count as real experience."

Lindsey Pollak, *Getting from College to Career*

and (2) that documenting your skills, knowledge, and traits within each "experience" (e.g., each separate "job") listed on your résumé is extremely important. The typical list of former jobs is never in itself adequate for a persuasive college résumé. That list is only a start, merely a part of your Masterlist. And it needs to be tweaked for each audience anyway. Be specific. Document what you learned that would likely be relevant to the organization and position you seek.

⚲ *Résumé Excerpt*

Paid Work Experiences

EXPERIENCE
Sales Associate, **Debbie's Spoil-Your-Tots Shop, Washington, DC (9/XX–5/XX)**
- Specialized in explaining and demonstrating the practical and safety features of dozens of child car seat products
- Recognized as part-time employee of the month
- Trained my replacement and provided ongoing support after leaving position
- Mastered proprietary database inventory and ordering system

Counselor, **Camp Kladder, Tollsma, MI (summer 20XX)**
- Counseled 12 campers, ages 7–16, in weekly residential camp
- Taught 3 skills classes each weekday, including public speaking, computing, and digital photography

The word "proprietary" indicates that the software was specific to the organization, not a well-known, off-the-shelf product. If you've mastered such software, you've had to learn it from scratch. This requires more computer savvy than just using software you learned at home or in school.

Note that these paid experiences focus the résumé on *relational* and *technological* skills, the traits of caring and self-motivation, and technical knowledge.

You can avoid the job-equals-experience trap by legitimately including a broader range of skills, knowledge, and traits under "experience." So as you review your Masterlist material, don't limit

📖 *Expert Advice*

Include Non-Robotic Activities

The "activities" section of a résumé is where you "let the reader know you're more than a robot that does nothing but work and study."

D. A. Hayden and Michael Wilder,
From B.A. to Payday

your résumé selections to full-time *paid* employment. Also consider as experience:

- **Interning**—paid or nonpaid "work" for both for-profit and nonprofit organizations—whether or not for academic credit—that resulted in your learning about the organization and the kind of work performed there, as well as about yourself

- **Volunteering**—projects or special activities in which you were involved, probably on behalf of nonprofit organizations such as community, educational, professional, governmental, and religious groups; this can include service-learning projects on behalf of a college or university

- **Self-employment**—including freelance work done for others, also known as "independent contracting" or just "contracting," where you might have been paid per project rather than an hourly rate, and where you acted as the head of your own business by recruiting one or more clients, managing your schedule, negotiating a fee or hourly rate, billing the client(s), and completing the project per client specifications or desires

Again, the key is that you *learned something* as an intern, volunteer, or self-employed (contract) worker. You gained experience. It's not enough to say that you were simply a member of an organization unless you can document how you served the organization and what you learned as a result. Be prepared. If you don't ask yourself the following questions, one of your interviewers eventually will: "Why did you put this on your résumé?" "What did you accomplish for the organization?" If you can't give solid answers in terms of skills, knowledge, or traits, then don't include the question-eliciting item on your résumé until you can!

"Official" internships and titled volunteer experiences for which you may have received academic credit are more impressive than non-titled, unofficial work listed on your résumé. But any internship experience can be valuable if you're open to learning. Even just observing what goes on in an organization can benefit you and your future employers. This is why you need to document what you *know*, as well as what you've *done*, in the positions you've held. Otherwise internship entries, in particular, can resemble mere "gofer" work—"go for this" and "go for that."

Résumé Excerpt

Intern and Volunteer Experiences

EXPERIENCE
Worship Committee Member, **Hicks Community Church (9/XX–5/XX)**
- Presented monthly youth group plans to the music committee
- Collaborated weekly with pastor and other members to create youth-engaging, visually vibrant worship services

Marketing Intern, **Dekker Vocational College (spring 20XX)**
Freelance Designer **(summer 20XX)**
- Assisted graphic designer by securing and reviewing 6 competitive quotes for printing single-color and full-color brochures
- Wrote copy for and proofread two recruiting brochures distributed to high schools

Camp Counselor, **Camp Burley Bum-Bum (summer 20XX)**
- Co-counseled and provided 24-hour care for 20 campers, ages 7–16
- Taught 3 daily skills classes, including arts, crafts, and digital photography

Note that the above experiences focus the résumé on skills and knowledge in visual arts, along with the relational traits.

As for the sticky issue of leaving a job after a short time, there are a few things to consider. If it was a short-duration job and you had a good reason for leaving, such as a sudden layoff or unexpected illness, or if you quickly discovered that the job was not a good fit, you might not have to include this in the résumé. Twice in my life I worked for two days at jobs before realizing that they were not what I had expected and that I was the wrong person for them. One of them was working on a city garbage truck; my back couldn't take the lifting of heavy trash into the truck. The other was a union apprenticeship in a narrow electronics field that didn't have enough intellectual stimulation to keep me interested in the tasks.

In both cases the employers understood why I was leaving, and I didn't accept any wages. If I had been filling out a comprehensive job application shortly after those experiences, I might have been obligated to include the experiences, although not having been compensated for the work suggests that I was not employed. If I had worked for weeks with compensation, however, I definitely would have been obligated to include those experiences on an application and résumé as long as the position was relatively recent (say, sometime within the last two to three years). Obviously these are ethical judgments, and there are no hard-and-fast rules about including short-term work on résumés.

If you were on a job longer than a few months, and your reason for leaving was not so noble—such as being fired—include the job on your résumé and be prepared to answer questions about why you left and what you learned from the experience. If you can explain briefly why you were let go and what you've learned as a result, you might want to include that explanation on your résumé. Also, chances are that you made positive contributions to the organization even though you were eventually terminated. Be sure to focus on your positive contributions, not just on self-improvements you made after you were fired.

Sometimes people are terminated for refusing to do things that conflict with their consciences. Or because they have allowed themselves to become overextended and are unable to satisfactorily juggle all of their responsibilities. Or because, as an employee, they resisted new organizational policies, work hours, or job duties. Or because of extended illness. Or because of personality conflicts with coworkers or supervisors. The reasons are varied and frequently mixed, if not complicated. Employers know this. They're not expecting perfection. Employers look favorably on applicants who know their weaknesses as well as their strengths and who are mature enough to address their weaknesses while leveraging their strengths. Just consider the euphemistic, nuanced language used to describe terminations: canned, dumped, dismissed, ousted, shown the door, downsized, recycled, eliminated, jettisoned, given the heave-ho, laid off, let go, not reappointed, and on and on. Each word or phrase suggests particular connotations. Terminations are rarely simple. Sometimes employers and employees perceive the same facts very differently.

℞ Résumé Excerpt

Resignation

EXPERIENCE
Sixth Grade Teacher, **Wilson Elementary School**
(9/XX–12/XX)
- Taught science, coached soccer, developed new parent-teacher communication policies
- Resigned at the end of first semester when extreme conflicts among the school board, administration, and union made it impossible for me to focus on teaching

Note that because this teacher left midyear, according to the dates of employment, and teacher contracts are normally for full years, an explanation was probably important for this résumé, even though reasons for leaving positions are not required on résumés. Sometimes the "reason for leaving" is required on job application forms. A past resignation or termination will usually be addressed in the first round of job interviews.

It's better to include a previous termination on your résumé rather than to have the subject come up unexpectedly at an inopportune time (like in the middle of an interview) and ruin your chances of securing the job. Some employers conduct pre-interview reference checks, online name searches, and legal due diligence. Of course the

Dr. Q's tip

Don't put "Education" before "Experience" in your résumé unless you are using the résumé for an academic purpose, such as a graduate school application. Why? Because an education-first résumé screams out:

"MERE STUDENT!"

expression "let go" is better than "fired," since the former can mean anything from being replaced by the boss's kid to being the victim of organizational downsizing during tough economic times. The phrase "laid off" usually implies that the position itself was eliminated, that no one was going to be hired as a replacement. In some industries and professions, the majority of workers have been laid off at some point during their careers.

Summarize Your Education

In most cases, the importance of your education for composing a résumé isn't simply the degree you earned but what you learned along the way. Even for professional degrees in high-demand fields, such as accounting and engineering, broadening the educational section of your résumé is essential for highlighting a wider range of skills, knowledge, and traits than those merely suggested by the degree itself.

If you graduated from a college or university within the last two years, round out your educational experiences with special aspects of your college activities, not with routine academic requirements, expected courses, and predictable projects. For instance, the fact that a college biology major completed a list of standard biology courses is both common sense and a waste of résumé space. If the same biology major interned for a summer in a biological context, paid or unpaid, the special work should be included under "Education." Similarly, a biology course research paper that received a strong evaluation from a professional should be included on a science-focused résumé unless the job seeker has more significant, job-related experience.

If you're an upcoming or very recent college graduate, you'll probably need to fall back on some school-related experiences for your résumé. Go back to your Masterlist and strengthen your list of school activities. Jog your memory with a copy of your college grade transcript, textbooks, and any course files or notebooks. The following questions will help you expand your college-related Masterlist material and produce an impressive résumé that goes beyond "education as usual."

Special Features of Your School

What are your college or university's distinct mission and purpose? How are they translated into your education? For instance, does the school emphasize any of the following?

- Service learning (academic "credit" for volunteer work)
- Character formation
- Broad-based liberal arts education ("general education" courses and experiences in addition to specialized courses in your major)
- Leadership training courses, activities, or positions (on or off campus)
- Extensive, across-the-curriculum writing or speaking experience
- Cross-cultural experiences (urban, rural, or international)
- Environmental awareness/learning
- Research opportunities with professors or other staff members
- Technology skills, including special hardware or software incorporated in class work
- The study of other languages/cultures (particularly through off-campus travel and programs)
- Interesting special-term courses (e.g., January terms; May terms;

Dr. Q's tip

Generally speaking, even if you are a recent college graduate, don't include your cumulative grade point average (GPA) on your résumé unless it's spectacular, such as a 3.7 or 3.8 average on a 4.0-point scale. Few employers really care about your GPA unless it reflects a stellar academic career or if you graduated recently and lack other job-performance data. In the latter case, if you don't include a GPA on your résumé you'll probably be asked about it at the first interview, just to make sure you weren't a substandard student.

Grade inflation has turned nearly all students into "better-than-average" achievers. High school GPAs are even less meaningful than those from college, and graduate school GPAs are rarely cited.

A graduate degree is more important than the GPA you earned. Attending college or graduate school is a plus on a résumé, even if you never completed your degree. Indicate when and where you attended and what you studied.

Nevertheless, if your GPA in your academic major was exceptional, you can include that instead of a weaker cumulative GPA. Most college transcripts indicate both cumulative and academic-major GPAs.

summer sessions; and other short, intensive terms between semesters or quarters)
- Extracurricular requirements
- Sports participation (extracurricular or collegiate)
- Residential life leadership (in dorms, private living arrangements, sororities or fraternities, etc.)

If you're not sure about your school's distinctive features, check out its website and course catalog. Examine the school's mission statement. How does it describe the school's emphases? Also examine the website for your own major or department within the school. What are the department's particular foci, goals, and features? This kind of school-related research is particularly important if your college is not well known or if you'll be applying for positions in a region distant from where your school is located. Be prepared to include on your résumé any distinctives of the school or department that may be relevant to specific jobs.

Suppose you earned an education degree from a medium-sized, Midwestern liberal arts college that emphasizes "social engagement." Chances are that some of the schools to which you would apply for teaching jobs will have a similar focus. When that's the case, highlight your college experience in those résumés.

You would still mention the school's focus in your other résumés, but you wouldn't concentrate on the theme of social engagement. Even if your school doesn't have a carefully integrated educational curriculum, you might be surprised to discover that administrators and faculty use a range of specific experiences to create a particular educational approach. Schools offer general-education courses, residential requirements, cross-cultural experiences, internships, co-op programs, campus lectures, arts events, and many more

📖 *Expert Advice*

Emphasize "Education" for School-Based Jobs

"If you are applying for academic jobs such as college library positions, list your 'education' information before other categories and experience."

Rachel Applegate, "Résumés and Cover Letters (For Library Employment)," *Indiana Libraries* activities to distinguish themselves from other colleges. So determine how your school's educational and extracurricular offerings can help you demonstrate your value to particular employers.

Uncommon Educational Opportunities or Accomplishments

What did you study, learn, and experience that will distinguish you from other students at your school or in your major? For example, did you do any of the following?

- Finish any special-topic, non-required courses
- Complete a second major or minor program
- Undertake an independent study with a teacher
- Attend special seminars, presentations, or conferences
- Spend a term off campus, perhaps in a different cultural or urban setting
- Conduct research for a professor (if the professor acted as a supervisor, you should include his or her name in your résumé)

Course-Related Accomplishments

What did you do within specific courses that is particularly notable or at least illustrates your skills, knowledge, or traits? Consider such course-related activities as these:

- Time-intensive or complex course projects
- Speeches, individual presentations, or productions
- Research papers or studies
- Group work, group presentations, or other collaborative learning
- Extensive reviews of any books, articles, or online sources
- Theses, performances, or productions

Expert Advice 📖

Highlight College Research Projects

"If you've been involved in undergraduate research, briefly describe that research in your résumé. It documents that you learned more than most students about a subject."

Stephen Jones, "How to Create a Winning Résumé," *The Black Collegian*

📖 *Expert Advice*

Include Relevant Personal Interests

"Although employers value work-related skills, some students—particularly those with limited experience—may draw upon personal interests, hobbies, and family life to identify relevant skills. The key is to demonstrate how the skills are transferable to the potential job situation."

Karl L. Smart, "Articulating Skills in the Job Search," *Business Communication Quarterly*

Campus Leadership Positions

Usually the best place to list high-responsibility campus leadership activities on a résumé is under "Education." But in a few cases you can include campus leadership under "Experience." For instance, if you were a resident adviser in a dormitory, an elected official for a campus organization, or served on the staff of the campus yearbook or newspaper, you could include those activities as "Experience" rather than just "Education" (academic study), depending upon the extent and value of the work for a specific résumé.

Keep in mind the ultimate test for any official positions or titles you have held: If you didn't do anything in the position (e.g., if it was merely a title without any responsibilities or accomplishments), or if what you accomplished doesn't seem worth sharing with others, you probably shouldn't list it—except possibly in the "Activities" category. One exception is honorary titles you received as acknowledgements of your efforts or accomplishments.

What if you never graduated or are still in school, perhaps pursuing a degree part-time or taking a semester or two off to earn additional money to pay for more education? First, ask yourself whether you really intend to complete your college education, and, if so, when this is realistically likely to happen. Indicate on your résumé your expected date of completion [e.g., B.A. in Philosophy, Arizona College, Green, AZ (Expected May 20XX)]. This is both honest and helpful to employers. If you recently completed some college courses but don't plan to continue your education in the near future, follow the same guidelines as for graduates, highlighting your education under a separate category.

If you took college courses more than five years ago and never graduated, summarize your work in a brief "Education" category at the end of your résumé. After all, you still benefit from the education you

๏ *Résumé Excerpt*

Personalized Education Experiences

EDUCATION
B.S. in Computer Science, Jager University, Downer, IL (May 20XX)
- Completed extensive writing program and public speaking requirements
- Collaborated with small group to design award-winning senior project
- Conducted usability study for class project on designing cell phone technologies for busy travelers
- Earned service-learning credit for setting up multi-platform computer network for nonprofit community group

Note that these kinds of personalized experiences convey a well-rounded education and express traits such as self-initiative, commitment, and an entrepreneurial spirit.

have received. Today some students discontinue college simply because of cost. Also, don't assume that you'll never complete your degree. For one thing, some of the new online and local degree-completion programs accept older college credits and life experience toward their degree requirements. For another, college dropouts often re-enroll when they discover that their employer will pay for them to complete their education. Or because their spouses are employed by a college that pays for a spouse's tuition. You never know!

List Your Activities

This last category is an opportunity for you to include materials relevant to a specific audience that don't fit under either of the first two categories ("Experience" and "Education"). This is a flexible and important third topic for career seekers, one that will enable you to include just about anything that documents your skills, knowledge, and traits relative to a particular résumé for a specific audience.

Dr. Q's tip

Don't include an item just because it supposedly will "look good on a résumé." You might be asked about it during an interview. Include items that you know will help you demonstrate why you're the right person for a particular position and/or for a specific organization (remember the key words and phrases the profession uses, as demonstrated in want ads and the like). You're far better off fine-tuning the ways you express activities than trying to create a positive impression by listing items that didn't really require your own extensive involvement, effort, or learning.

Nevertheless, there's a catch: To as great a degree as possible, include only items that indicate what you have *actively* accomplished. Avoid entries such as meaningless organizational memberships for which you did nothing but join or pay your dues. You'll probably have to make some tough decisions about what not to include. The rule of thumb is to use the "Activities" category to further document some of your specific skills, knowledge, and traits for a particular audience. In other words, the material in this category is likely to change significantly from résumé to résumé, interview to interview, across different organizations or even within the same organization if significant time has passed or your job has changed. Below are some potentially persuasive activities to consider. They are stated specifically to highlight ongoing activity.

Community Involvement
Note the specific frequency of each activity in the entries below.

- Serving on 3 active community committees
- Organizing monthly neighborhood meetings to address community issues
- Mentoring kids or adults weekly, either one-on-one or in groups
- Teaching adults English or life skills 1 evening weekly
- Tutoring students after school twice weekly
- Assisting disabled persons, shut-ins, or the elderly 2 or 3 times monthly

Hobbies
Note especially those that show particular skills, knowledge, or traits:

- Teamwork or organizational abilities gained through sports participation, coaching, training, and organizing
- Musical study and/or performance, particularly over an extended period of five or more consecutive years
- Collecting cultural artifacts, particularly if the activity involves research, self-study, buying and selling or trading, and promotion
- Studying social or cultural phenomena, such as particular life-styles and generational trends
- Extensive travel, along with the study and experience of other cultures
- Reading in specific areas, such as literature, history, or current affairs
- Firsthand, nature-related skills or knowledge, including that gained from regular outdoor activities such as gardening, boating, hiking, and birding
- Technological skills developed and employed in conjunction with avocational pursuits, from blogging, photography, and website design to multimedia editing

If you have enough material from your Masterlist, you can limit this category to activities that fit a particular job-focused résumé. In that case, you might consider naming the category "Related Activities" to emphasize this point. But remember that if your civic involvement or hobbies have led to completed projects directly related to the purpose for the specific résumé, you might instead include them under "Experience."

Add Special Categories
Sometimes the three basic categories of Experience, Education, and Activities are insufficient. Suppose you have relevant material that doesn't fit well into any one of the three categories. You might strengthen your résumé by creating one or two additional categories

just by shifting a few entries from one or more of the other categories to a new one.

The two most impressive additional categories today involve *technology* and *culture* (especially languages and cross-cultural experience). These two areas open many doors for career seekers in the increasingly global, high-tech economy. If you have more than one or two items for these categories, it makes sense to highlight technology and culture separately.

⚲ *Résumé Excerpt*

Common Additional Category—Technology

TECHNOLOGY
- Proficient in Microsoft Word, PowerPoint, Excel, Access, Outlook, and Publisher
- Experienced at setting up, using, and troubleshooting wireless/wired PC networks
- Knowledge of Mac and Windows OS
- Competent with Visual Basic
- Microsoft Network Certified

Note that the items listed above are standardized to begin with adjectives and nouns—not verbs.

The best section titles for technology are "Technology," "Computers," "Technological Experience," or "Technological Skills." In any case, if your abilities with new forms of communication, information, databases, computerized design, or other computer technologies are considerably above average, you probably should highlight them in a special category. You can determine whether your skills are significant based in part on the frequency of help requested of you by friends, family, and co-hobbyists. You might also demonstrate a technical aptitude by learning technological skills quickly on the job and helping coworkers to learn them as well. Self-taught skills show that you are self-motivated, a fast learner, and passionate about mastering such skills.

Yet another kind of technology-related skill is knowing how to use technologies appropriately in relationships with coworkers, clients, and customers. For instance, protecting the privacy of sensitive data in health care, human resources, and legal situations involves both ethical and legal knowledge. Similarly important is determining when to use a technology like e-mail to communicate with others and when it is preferable to interact in person. Employees' use of corporate technologies for personal business is a matter of good judgment, not just company policies.

℘ *Résumé Excerpt*

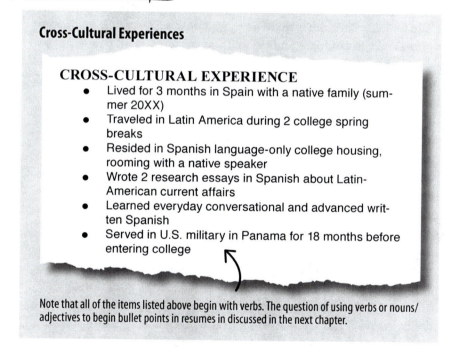

Cross-Cultural Experiences

CROSS-CULTURAL EXPERIENCE
- Lived for 3 months in Spain with a native family (summer 20XX)
- Traveled in Latin America during 2 college spring breaks
- Resided in Spanish language-only college housing, rooming with a native speaker
- Wrote 2 research essays in Spanish about Latin-American current affairs
- Learned everyday conversational and advanced written Spanish
- Served in U.S. military in Panama for 18 months before entering college

Note that all of the items listed above begin with verbs. The question of using verbs or nouns/adjectives to begin bullet points in resumes in discussed in the next chapter.

A résumé category labeled "Multicultural Experience" or "Cross-cultural Experience" can be similarly impressive in multicultural communities and a world economy. Add such a category if you have extensive experience living in other cultures and speaking a second language, including sign language. Be sure to document when and where you lived in another culture, the extent of your ability to speak

Dr. Q's tip

If you include obscure awards or honors on your résumé, briefly describe what they mean, such as, "Received the Henry J. Molder Award for excellence in local volunteer service."

and write in other languages, and opportunities you have had to use your cultural and linguistic knowledge to serve a diverse population. Perhaps you lived with someone from another culture. Maybe you have traveled extensively.

The value of diverse cultural experiences is twofold. First, you gain skill in and knowledge of other people's ways of life, from appropriate clothing and personal space to fundamentally different religious convictions or no such convictions whatsoever. Second, intercultural experience teaches us more about ourselves; we see more clearly who we are, what we believe, and how we act when we have an opportunity to compare and/or contrast ourselves with people from other cultures. Much of what modern businesses and nonprofit organizations do today requires cross-cultural activities, both within and beyond the organizational framework.

A third possible supplemental category for college résumé writers can be called "Honors" or "Awards and Honors." Few college students or recent graduates have enough items to warrant a separate category, so it's usually best to include notable recognitions in one of the three major categories: college-related scholarships and other recognitions under "Education"; work-related distinctions under "Experience"; and others, especially those stemming from sports, cultural or artistic activities, and hobbies, under "Activities."

Creating a special category just for one or two common awards that are not particularly noteworthy actually calls attention to the fact that you have not been recognized for extraordinary accomplishments. As with less-than-sterling grade point averages and mixed employee reviews, it's best not to try to put a better spin on the facts. Focus on your documentable strengths—not on stretching your less notable achievements.

Conclusion

There's a scene in *Ocean's Eleven* where Brad Pitt is giving final instructions to Matt Damon. Pitt says, "Don't, under any circumstances…"—and then gets cut off. The audience wonders what critical advice Pitt's character had intended to pass on. Damon is sent off on his first major heist without his mentor's last-minute guidance. Not a good situation.

Now if I were the more experienced Pitt and you were the novice Damon, about to begin your résumé-writing mission, here's how I would finish that statement: "Don't, under any circumstances, *submit a generic résumé.*" Generic résumés produce unsuccessful career-seeking missions.

As human resources directors have consistently told me, interview-generating résumés match the applicant's experiences to the specific skills, knowledge, and traits required for particular positions. The applicant doesn't necessarily have to possess all of the "desired" qualifications. But the aspiring worker does need to demonstrate in the résumé that he or she knows what's required for the position. The applicant must match some of his or her experiences to the particular position, using fitting language from the job description, classified advertisement, or organizational website. This will greatly increase the number of interviews you generate. If not, your résumé will probably be lost in the pile of similarly generic efforts circulated by hasty job seekers.

What to Do Now

As you begin filling in your résumé categories with relevant material from your Masterlist, your résumé will start looking persuasive—even to yourself! Continue jumping back and forth between your Masterlist and your developing résumé, identifying experiences that convincingly demonstrate what you have to offer by way of skills, knowledge, and traits. Remember to review (and use as appropriate) the specific career-related language you've learned from the classified ads, career professionals, and other research.

In the next chapter, I'll explain how to fine-tune the material in each of these categories. I'll also show you how to write a summary statement. Soon your résumé will be rising to the top of employers' piles. Your résumés will be generating serious attention—and you'll be scheduling interviews.

Fine-Tune Your Résumé

In this chapter you'll learn:

How to write a convincing summary statement
How to use persuasive, honest, carefully crafted language
How to format entries under each category
How to make your résumé digitally scannable

In the process of reviewing résumés submitted to me for a part-time professional position in copywriting, my attention was caught by one in particular. The layout was exceptional, including adequate white space, a laser-printed and highly readable text, a helpful summary statement at the top, and an impressive list of past employment positions, duties, and accomplishments. But none of those admirable qualities impressed me as much as this one: the self-proclaimed "detail-oriented" copywriter had missed numerous misspellings and stylistic inconsistencies. His résumé looked great but contradicted his claim to be a careful copywriter.

How does this kind of sloppiness slip by us? First, we all get tired and lose the concentration we need in order to review our own résumés over and over again. Second, we fail to recruit language-loving, nitpicky friends and colleagues to review our résumés. Third, we naively convince ourselves that all résumés include imprecise and incorrect language—and that employers are therefore quite forgiving. Actually, most employers tend to notice résumé mistakes, much as they would twelve-inch prickly weeds sprouting in the middle of closely cropped, verdant lawns. Fourth, college students in particular have a tendency to wait until the last minute to compose each résumé, rather than polishing a series of résumés that can be quickly fine-tuned for given positions.

Now is the time to begin polishing your résumé, transforming it into your own, well-crafted story, and nuancing it for various possible positions within your most promising career areas. You've already got the material you'll need for a persuasive résumé. (If not, just review the previous chapters!) You're ready to express yourself convincingly, carefully, and ethically. As I will explain next, begin your résumé with an attention-getting, position-focused summary. Then make sure your formatting is clean, clear, and consistent. Finally, verify that your résumé is ready to be scanned into the databases of larger organizations and online job-hunting services. The end is in sight!

Use a Summary Statement

One traditional way to begin your résumé material, immediately beneath your name and contact information, is with an *objective statement*. An objective statement expresses what you want to "get" from those who read your résumé. According to this approach, your résumé content begins with a response to a want ad headline. Suppose the ad headline read:

Wanted: Entry-Level Marine Biologist

You would then write the following objective statement:

OBJECTIVE: to gain an entry-level position in marine biology

Then all you need to do is tweak the objective statement for each application, right? Wrong.

While an objective statement can be read speedily by busy employers, it's not particularly persuasive. It doesn't indicate what you *offer*—only what you *want*. On the positive side, an objective can help a reader identify the position(s) for which to consider you. In most cases, however, your cover letter can accomplish that purpose even more precisely. In addition, all objective statements tend to read alike, with little or no distinction. Objective statements don't even hint at your skills, knowledge, and traits. This is why I'm not a big fan of objective statements. Many employers aren't impressed by them, either. In fact, the clear trend is away from generic objective statements and toward applicant-specific, position-focused summary statements that include an objective.

A satisfactory summary statement will be a little longer than an objective statement. But it will also be more informative and time saving for employers. If written concisely, geared toward a specific career and position (sometimes even a particular employer), and focused on your job-related skills, knowledge, and traits, a summary statement will almost always get your résumé noticed. More potential employers will peruse your résumé. A solid summary statement will also significantly increase your interview chances. Finally, a well-written summary will increase your odds of being considered for other positions at the same company. Why? Because employers will immediately see connections between your skills, knowledge, and traits and other open positions within the organization. If you use only an objective statement and that specific position is no longer available, the employer is unlikely to even glance at the rest of your résumé.

It helps to think of your résumé's summary statement as a news headline. Every good headline points the reader to the "who, what, where, when, why, and how" of the full news story published beneath the headline: "President tells nation to conserve energy." Then there might be a subhead: "Encourages citizens to reduce demand."

Now imagine a headline for your résumé, something like: "New economist offers services to needy banks." Let's add the following subhead: "Seeks to serve with skills, knowledge, and traits." These two "headers" could summarize a news report about a recent college graduate in economics who has some specific skills, knowledge, and traits

Expert Advice

Leisure-Services Résumés

"In the growing field of recreation and leisure services, employers accept résumés: (1) with or without objective statements, (2) with or without college grads, (3) with references included, and (4) with one or more pages."

Craig M. Ross and Sarah J. Young, "Résumé Preferences: Is It Really 'Business as Usual'?" *Journal of Career Development*

📖 *Expert Advice*

Begin with a Servant Attitude

Your goal should be "to start your résumé with a focus on the employer and his or her needs. Tell readers what you can do for them."

Jay Conrad Levinson and David E. Perry, *Guerilla Marketing for Job Hunters 2.0*

that might contribute to the success of particular banks. The headers also indicate what the new economist desires—to serve a bank.

Now compare the fictional headlines with the following résumé objective statement: "Position in Banking Economics." That kind of tersely worded objective statement doesn't say much of anything about the applicant; it's thoroughly generic, without a subhead and lacking a related "story"—your own.

So why do college students write such nondescript, self-serving objective statements? Probably because they automatically mimic the few résumés they've seen. Also, they fear composing an inappropriate résumé and thereby reducing their job prospects. Because college students don't see many actual résumés, they believe the word-of-mouth "wisdom" about what makes for a solid résumé. Finally, college students use such objective statements because they're simple to compose and don't require self-knowledge, let alone knowledge about particular positions. Just fill in the blank: "Objective: An entry-level position in_____." What could be easier? But what could be less persuasive?

The biggest problem with objective statements is that they don't help career seekers to think in terms of serving an organization with their own unique combination of skills, knowledge, and traits. They allow career seekers to be lazy about their strengths and to avoid researching real career opportunities within an ever-changing job market. Objective statements even lull career seekers into forgetting that a résumé should serve the employer, not just the applicant. A summary statement better helps the employer make the right decisions about who can best serve the organization.

Consider what an objective statement says to potential employers. It tells them you're trying to get something *from* them: Gimme! Gimme! Gimme that job! By contrast, a summary statement, rightly focused on what you have to offer, helps the reader to recognize almost immediately the potential you have to serve the organization—not just what you want from it. Expressed honestly and concisely, a summary enables you to make your case on behalf of the employer as well as for the benefit of your career. Solid summary statements are a win-win proposition for you and a potential employer.

Objective statements do have their place. If an organization receives a lot of unsolicited résumés for many positions, its staff needs the ability to readily identify the job you're applying for. Larger employers, in particular, don't want to have to read through hundreds of résumés and/or examine hundreds of cover letters to determine which position an applicant seeks. Sometimes sizeable organizations go so far as to assign every job opening a special code number and to require applicants to use that code in all correspondence—even on résumés.

Still, summary statements can do double duty by identifying the position you seek *and* by distinguishing you from other applicants. With a little creative writing, they can include your career objective without coming across as self-serving. Such statements give you a golden opportunity to tell your story persuasively in a single sentence. The employer learns what you want *and* what you have to offer. More specifically, the employer can see immediately how your goal fits the organization's needs.

Compare this objective statement with the summary that follows:

OBJECTIVE: to gain an entry-level position in marine biology

SUMMARY: A hard-working marine biologist with cross-cultural experience and collaborative research skills seeks to contribute to the success of a marine organization committed to environmental stewardship.

Expert Advice 📖

Use Precise Objective Statements

"In career fields that prefer résumés with objective statements rather than summary statements, be sure to write a *specific* rather than a *general* objective statement. Tune your objective to the specific field and even to the particular job."

Peg Thoms, et. al., "Résumé Characteristics as Predictors of an Invitation to Interview," *Journal of Business and Psychology*

Or consider this summary for a different profession:

> **SUMMARY: A conscientious, dependable economist with strong interpersonal skills and extensive database abilities desires to serve a governmental agency's consumer affairs division.**

Your first reaction to these summaries is probably disbelief, if not intimidation. You might wonder if there really are college students or recent graduates who could claim these summary statements as honest expressions of what they have to offer. Do the statements suggest to you that the résumé writers are merely boasting? That they think too highly of themselves?

Don't worry. If you look closely at these summary statements you'll see that they are not outlandish, even for recent college graduates, as long as the rest of their résumé supports their claims about themselves. These and all other good summary statements contain three critical elements, usually in the following order:

1. **Demonstrable traits** (e.g., hardworking, conscientious)
2. **Demonstrable skills and knowledge** (e.g., research, computers, relationships)
3. **Desire to serve a particular kind of organization** (Why else would you apply?)

The key to successfully using a summary statement is *basing it on evidence in the résumé itself.* That's why it's a summary, not self-flattery. In over 30 years of working with college students, I've heard of only one instance in which a potential employer rejected someone's application because it included a summary statement. In that case, the potential employer actually berated the applicant during an interview, claiming that the summary demonstrated immaturity and arrogance. Ironically, other prospective employers loved the same résumé, with the identical summary statement. Such is life! No one can please every employer all the time. But with an honest, clearly expressed summary statement, you'll please a greater number of employers more frequently. And you'll generate far more interviews.

If your résumé with a summary statement doesn't garner instant results, don't assume the problem is the statement itself. Presumably you've checked with one or more persons in the field about using a summary statement. If not, do so! At most, refine the summary statement for each position, unless you determine from professionals in your particular field of interest that a summary is not as appropriate as an objective statement.

Always write your summary statement *after* you've completed your Masterlist and a position-specific rough draft of your résumé that highlights your skills, knowledge, and traits. As long as your summary statement is defensible, you have nothing to worry about. The strengths of a summary statement far surpass the weaknesses. See appendix C for help writing one.

Expert Advice 📖

Express Your Geographic Flexibility

"Fortune 500 organizations do not find high school accomplishments or information important for college graduates' résumés, but they do indicate that an applicant should express a willingness to relocate or travel."

Kevin L. Hutchinson and Diane S. Brefka, "Personnel Administrators' Preferences for Résumé Content: Ten Years After," *Business Communication Quarterly*

By writing a solid summary statement you'll be serving busy and not-so-busy employers alike. If you're uncomfortable with the idea of using a seemingly self-promotional summary statement, remember that a defensible summary serves your potential employer. It provides a quick overview of your life story, as fleshed out in your résumé. Yes, a summary statement is somewhat self-promotional. So what? Get over it! As a college student or recent graduate, you need to learn to sell both your abilities and your character in the job market. Honest persuasion is one means toward getting interviews—and eventually a career-worthy job.

But what if you're a very recent college graduate or even a university senior? What if you're fresh out of school and applying for a job in a field that's different from your major? In these cases, aren't you being unethical if you claim in a summary statement to already be a professional? Generally speaking, you become a "professional" once you begin working within your field. For instance, a student teacher is already teaching. Someone who sculpts is a sculptor. A friend of mine

📖 *Expert Advice*

Release Hot Air

Your résumé should "communicate your value and enthusiastically engage the reader, not provide a long-winded, never-ending biography of your professional life."

Jay A. Block, *101 Best Ways to Land a Job in Troubled Times*

who is a Hollywood film producer says that the only requirement for becoming a producer is printing business cards that say "Producer." He's only half joking. Today even middle school students are producing their own films for YouTube.

Of course in some fields, such as law and audiology, where college graduates generally have to earn a graduate degree in order to practice, the situation is more complicated. Abraham Lincoln never attended law school, even though he was a practicing attorney. Yet today about half a dozen American states allow people to practice law by passing the bar exam, even if they never attended law school. Of course, you shouldn't claim to be an attorney on the basis of having completed a pre-law under-graduate degree. Nevertheless, don't underestimate the progress you've already made professionally through schooling, internships, related part-time job experience, volunteer experiences, and the like. On the one hand, don't boast. Be mindful of formal professional titles and required credentials. But don't undervalue yourself and your experience. An undergraduate student is not automatically an attorney, but a writer is a writer regardless of degrees and titles. At some point you'll have to stop calling yourself a student and begin calling yourself a professional.

🔅 *Dr. Q's tip*

In your résumé, use the past tense for completed activities and the present tense for current activities. If you have completed some tasks and are still engaged in others at the same organization, you might want to use only the present tense for all of the bulleted items related to that particular organization.

In a summary, you can always soften your personal claims about yourself by using adjectives such as "new," "beginning," and "student": "A new audiologist who loves to make money and wants her own corporate business cards and spacious office seeks an entry-level position to begin climbing the ladder of success." Granted, this summary is over the top. But you get the idea.

Résumé Excerpt

Summary Statement

J. R. Russboom Jr.

SUMMARY
A conscientious, dependable writer with strong interpersonal skills and extensive computer abilities desires to serve a public relations agency specializing in nonprofit work.

EXPERIENCE
Intern, DeWyn Media Agency (formerly Epiphony Communications), Coldest, Alberta (summer 20XX)
- Wrote copy for 6 eight-page, in-house client newsletters
- Copyedited dozens of press releases, including complete fact-checking
- Drafted phone messages from clients for head of agency and represented agency at over a dozen pro bono community events

EDUCATION
B.A., Public Relations, Loder University, Fuller, ND (May 20XX)
- Completed semester-in-Sweden program at Freeberg University
- Copyedited weekly campus paper 3 semesters
- Transcribed phone messages and executed client call-backs for agency head
- Voluntarily helped professor create multimedia PowerPoint presentations for use in 6 news reporting classes

ACTIVITIES
- Tutored middle-school children weekly in computer use at inner-city Rooks-Westra School
- Attended monthly luncheons with nonprofit public relations mentoring group

Use Words Honestly and Well

Your résumé can't create itself. If you conscientiously maintain a Masterlist, you'll always have more information than you can possibly cover in a one- or two-page résumé. You'll have to decide what to include and how to express yourself in each résumé for each job. So there really is no ultimate "objectivity" when it comes to composing a résumé. But you still need to use words honestly, not just persuasively. After all, honesty is an outstanding trait. Why not demonstrate in the résumé that you exemplify the trait? You can do so by using language wisely and well, not just by avoiding technically inaccurate statements. Here's how:

Use Strong Action Verbs

Your résumé documents your actions—what you have accomplished or are accomplishing. Therefore, you should use concrete, action-oriented verbs. "Have taken" is not as good as "took" phone messages. "Did editing" is not as strong as "edited" or, if you are currently doing it, "editing." Show that you're a doer rather than just a talker by employing the most fitting action-oriented verbs. This technique might help you: Call up a mental image when you visualize yourself "doing" the verb. The more concrete and action-oriented the image, the more accurate and honest the verb (see appendix D for a list of action verbs).

Choose Precise Verbs and Nouns

Select words that are concrete rather than overly general. Be as precise as possible with both verbs and nouns. For instance, college students who have worked as restaurant hosts or servers often include an entry line like this on their résumé:

- Dealt with lots of difficult customers

Undoubtedly so. We've all witnessed irate diners in action. But what does the phrase "dealt with" actually mean? Did you tell them off? Show them the door? Ignore them for the rest of their meal? How many customers is "lots"? What made the customers "difficult" in the first place—your poor service!? In contrast, consider the following concrete language:

- Satisfied hundreds of challenging customers monthly, including on-the-go lunch patrons

Chances are this revision is more accurate and more honest, as well as more persuasive. A savvy, experienced server learns how to satisfy the diverse needs of social and business customers—not merely how to "deal" with angry or "difficult" people. There are many reasons why customers may be challenging. They may be excessively demanding because of their overblown expectations or unreasonable demands. Customers may be impatient if they're on a tight schedule. They may grow angry because of the mistakes of a cook, busser, or server. Satisfying a diverse clientele can really be challenging.

Dr. Q's tip

Begin every bulleted subpoint on your résumé with an action verb. Each carefully selected verb indicates not just *what* you did but also that you are a *doer*. These verbs can represent your skills, knowledge, and traits in action.

Of course, if you were a server and never did get the knack of how to satisfy customers during hectic meal hours, you shouldn't include a line like this in your résumé! But if you began as a server with rough edges and grew into a patron-serving, customer-appreciated, management-affirmed server, you acquired in the process various skills, knowledge, and traits that are transferable to many other careers. Still, you need to describe what you learned in order to list it effectively on your résumé. The more concisely and yet concretely you can express your work, the better (see appendix E on writing and editing concisely).

Determining the best verbs without overusing a handful of action words (like "helped," "organized," or "created") can be challenging. Yet it's essential to be as job-specific as possible. Use a thesaurus to find just the right verb for each bulleted line on your résumé. Most word processors include a weak but passable thesaurus feature. There are also online thesauruses available free of charge. A number of major book publishers offer outstanding thesauruses that organize words by broad concepts (e.g., by the concept of "assisted") rather than just by synonyms. My favorite is *Bartlett's Roget's Thesaurus*.

Appendix D includes a list of common résumé verbs to help you determine the

Expert Advice

Avoid Chatty Language

"Even if you're a 'people person' seeking a position in the highly interactive profession of nursing, be sure to avoid writing your résumé so informally that it strikes employers as unprofessional."

Sue Howell, "Résumé Do's and Don'ts," *Nursing*

most precise choices for items on your résumé. Use the list in conjunction with a thesaurus, as needed. As much as possible, avoid repeating the same verbs over and over again, even if they are job-specific. Since nearly every item in your list of bullet points under each résumé category (e.g., Experience, Education, and Activities) will begin with a verb, repetition will be obvious to readers. Be as precise as possible. If a particular verb seems to describe exactly what you did but you're not entirely sure, look up that verb in a dictionary to confirm your assumption. The key is what a reader will assume the word means, not what you personally think it means. Again, go back to the career-specific language you gleaned from want ads and interviews. If any of those verbs honestly describes what you did, use it.

⚲ *Résumé Excerpt*

Accomplishments and Awards

ACCOMPLISHMENTS AND AWARDS
- Brawley Scholar (one of top 40 academic scholars), October 20XX
- Ingram Press "Spectacular Senior," May 27, 20XX
- Third place in 24-Hour Film Festival, Wesley Art Festival, Fall 20XX
- Two-time winner of 44-Hour Film Festival, South Wesley University, Spring and Fall 20XX
- Dean's List, South Wesley University, Spring and Fall 20XX

Note that the listings in an "awards" section of a résumé do not normally require action verbs.

In a few cases you won't need to begin a résumé entry with a verb, simply because the particular item doesn't call for it. For instance, if you received numerous awards, you wouldn't have to list each one on a separate line and find a new verb to begin each line. Similarly, just listing degrees and special certifications is adequate. Use diverse, precise verbs as much as possible, but don't feel compelled to force every entry into a verb format.

Watch Your Adjectives and Adverbs

In order to write an honest, yet persuasive résumé, you'll sometimes need to modify nouns and verbs with concrete adjectives and adverbs. Appendix B provides a list of adjectives that can serve as positive traits. Suppose you wrote, "Did surveys for college statistics class." That's relevant but overly general and potentially misleading information. A prospective employer might understandably read that entry as a questionable claim. So you'll need to be more specific. How many surveys did you do? What does "did" mean—that you administered them, distributed them, collected them, and analyzed them? Did you "do" these surveys for a beginning or advanced statistics class? Did you do them on your own or with others? Consider this revision:

Dr. Q's tip

Be sure to determine whether your career of interest uses particular verbs to describe specific activities. If you haven't yet done so, consult want ads in trade journals or professional magazines, often available in libraries or online. As appropriate, use those distinct verbs or phrases on your résumé. However, don't use any unfamiliar verbs without first researching what they mean in terms of that career, not just what they mean in general.

> "Personally wrote, revised, administered, analyzed, and summarized the results of a random marketing survey of 200 college students for an advanced statistics class."

That single, concrete résumé item honestly (presumably!) and powerfully communicates your experience. An employer will immediately see that you accomplished a lot of specific things in one project. Moreover, a potential employer will get a more concrete sense of the particular skills you learned and the kind of person you are: self-motivated, organized, and project oriented. Finally, the employer will see that you have learned the professional language of survey research. The reality is that you didn't just "do" a survey.

📖 *Expert Advice*

Don't Pad It

"Questionable résumé 'padding' includes using keywords that don't reflect your actual experience and abilities. Such 'indirect résumé fraud' has become widely accepted but still raises significant ethical issues."

Nicole Amare and Alan Manning, "Writing for the Robot: How Employer Search Tools Have Influenced Résumé Rhetoric and Ethics," *Business Communication Quarterly*

Honesty demands, then, that you avoid personal claims that might be technically true but a bit deceptive. For instance, the word "personally" in the summary above describes the fact that you did all of the survey work on your own. What if you conducted the survey with others, such as for a class-required group project? Then you shouldn't use a word like "personally." Instead, include an adverb to clarify the fact that you worked with others. Perhaps you "collectively" conducted or even "co-conducted" the survey with a small group. Or maybe you did part of the survey on your own and would like to highlight that solo effort on your résumé, along with your group accomplishments ("coauthored" and "personally administered").

These are critically important distinctions because they tell contrasting stories about your role in the survey project. They even highlight different personal traits, such as your ability to work both independently and collaboratively. If you worked with a small group and divided up the tasks, you most likely became familiar with only one or two aspects of survey research. If you did all of the survey-related tasks on your own, you likely gained a solid overview of the entire process.

So use modifiers carefully. Be clear and direct, not wordy. Be truthful. Don't oversell or undersell your accomplishments. Remember that you'll probably be questioned in an interview about specific items on your résumé. Employers might check with your references to see whether you in fact did what you say you did. Say what you mean, and mean what you say.

Additional Ethical Considerations

■ Distinguish between full-time and part-time employment, as needed for clarity. If a job was full-time (usually 32 or more hours weekly), you don't need to specify this on your résumé; "full-time" is the assumed meaning of any listed job. Any part-time work or full-time volunteering should ordinarily be identified as such, if it is not already clear from the context or description.

- Use job titles that accurately reflect your level of responsibility, as well as your actions. Avoid using, or at least explain the use of, job titles you might have been given that are not typical for your actual level of work and responsibility.

- Although you can't possibly include everything listed on your Masterlist in your final résumé, you need to include any and all items employers or other audiences should know about you because these entries will greatly color their view of your relevant skills, knowledge, or traits. For instance, are there particular hobbies or volunteer experiences that really capture the kind of person you are? Were there college clubs or other non-academic activities in which you greatly excelled and which gave you considerable satisfaction? If so, consider mentioning them.

- If you worked or volunteered less than a full year for a particular organization, specify the month-by-month time period during which you worked or volunteered. You can use either names or numbers for months (e.g., "5/XX–9/XX" or "May XX–Sept. XX"). In either case, be consistent. You

Expert Advice 📖

Represent Yourself Fairly

"If your résumé includes overt misrepresentations of you and your experience, you're less likely to be considered for hiring. Being truthful or factual is not enough. Avoid any language that could be interpreted as a misrepresentation, including language about your past activities that seems merely to mimic the job description."

Jennifer L. Wood, James M. Schmidtke, and Diane L. Decker, "Lying on Job Applications: The Effects of Job Relevance, Commission, and Human Resource Management Experience, *Journal of Business and Psychology* could use "summer," too, since employers know the academic calendar.

■ If you didn't receive a title for a current or former position, ask your supervisor to suggest a reasonable title to include on your résumé. If your supervisor is unavailable, first check to see whether a title was listed in your contract, letter of appointment, or any performance evaluation. As a last resort, ask someone else in the field who can give you an appropriate title, based upon your description of your duties. For entry-level work, the words "assistant to," coupled with the title of your supervisor, will generally do the trick:

Assistant to Chief Chemist
Assistant to Store Manager
Assistant to Sports Editor

Format Entries

Carefully chosen words are not enough for a lucid, persuasive résumé. In addition, a résumé needs to be well formatted so that the layout, design, and organization communicate clearly. Think clean and professional, not fancy. You don't want the résumé to look sloppy or amateurish. You want it to be properly dignified, not gimmicky. There are so many different ways of formatting résumés that you can easily get confused because of seemingly conflicting rules. Also, there are hundreds of simple and elegant computer-based templates designed to make content-poor résumés appear substantial.

Nevertheless, there is only one basic résumé-formatting rule: Be consistent. Make sure all similar entries are formatted alike. If you maintain consistency, you can't go far astray. Your résumé will look professional and serve the audience without resorting to complicated, flashy, or clever techniques that could tarnish your budding professional image. Simple, straightforward formatting is a virtue in résumé writing. Only if you work in the arts, and especially in graphic design, should you fret about résumé graphics. Even then, however, your accompanying portfolio is more important artistically than your résumé itself.

℘ *Résumé Excerpt*

Résumé Formatting with Bullets

SUMMARY

An energetic, Spanish-speaking teacher who loves children and knows the latest reading pedagogies desires to serve 3rd or 4th graders in an urban community.

EXPERIENCE

Student Teacher, Stephen Rex Charter Academy, Dorchester, MA (fall 20XX)

- Taught 4th grade in a largely Hispanic school, achieving excellent supervisor evaluations
- Worked closely with a master teacher who is a native Spanish speaker
- Initiated successful twice-weekly, after-school Spanish tutoring program for 8 students with no background in Spanish

EDUCATION

B.A. Elementary Education (Spanish minor), Mishkin College, Bradenton, FL (May 20XX)

- Earned major and minor in 5 years with elementary teaching accreditation in language arts and Spanish
- Studied conversational Spanish full-time in Guatemala for 6 weeks
- Assisted Spanish college teacher voluntarily with 4 conversation groups of beginning Spanish students for a semester
- Wrote a weekly multiculturalism column for campus paper for a semester
- Completed group project on the latest reading pedagogies and personally presented summary to entire class

The traditional manner of formatting a résumé works well in nearly every situation. That's why I recommend it. Since I've used it repeatedly in this book, you've probably figured it out on your own. By way of review, it looks like the above résumé excerpt, with a summary statement included at the beginning.

Note the following in the above sample résumé material:

- Limited use of centered text (normally only for the material at the top)

- Minimal use of italics (normally only for position titles)

- Simple bullets to organize each supporting line (as I'll discuss later, you can also use paragraph formatting with periods or semicolons between items)

- Parentheses to capture sub-points within the text (such as dates)

- Uppercase text for the main category headers (you might try using "small caps" as well)

- Minimum of one line space between main categories

- Simple, clean, readable layout that normally works best with at least 1" and preferably 1.5" margins

- Fairly large, readable font (normally 11- or 12-point) for everything except your name (up to 14-point font)

- Single, common font style (e.g., Arial or Times New Roman)

- Consistently formatted dates that do not add an extra line to an entry

- Minimal use of bolded text applied consistently throughout (usually only for name, categories, and sometimes position titles if they are important and not italicized)

Note that résumé entries are listed in reverse chronological order (the most recent items first) within categories. This not only makes it easy for a reader to review the life experiences embedded in the résumé but also accentuates your most recent work, activities, and education. There are ways of organizing items by other kinds of subheads, such as by skill sets, but they rarely work well for college students and recent graduates; they're also harder to write well and invite excessive repetition.

Some résumés use short paragraphs instead of bulleted lists. The above résumé would be the same in the paragraph format except that the bullet points would be strung together with semicolons or periods. Although the paragraph format is widely used, I believe that it's less effective for gaining the interest of hasty or busy readers. In fact, I think paragraph formatting is becoming less and less effective in the

℗ *Résumé Excerpt*

Résumé Formatting with Paragraphs

EXPERIENCE
Student Teacher, **Stephen Rex Charter Academy, Dorchester, MA (fall 20XX)**
> Achieved excellent evaluations teaching 4th grade in mainly Hispanic school. Taught alongside Spanish speaking master teacher. Initiated a successful Spanish tutoring program for 8 students with no background in Spanish.

EDUCATION
B.A. Elementary Education (Spanish minor), Mishkin College, Bradenton, FL (May 20XX)
> Earned elementary teaching accreditation in language arts and Spanish; developed language skills during study in Guatemala; aided Spanish professor with conversation groups of beginning students; wrote multiculturalism column for campus paper; presented group project summary on the latest reading pedagogies to entire class.

age of instant blogging, on-the-fly text messaging, and tweeting. Readers like concise wording with plenty of white space. Nevertheless, consider using paragraph formatting if you have a lot of relevant material (e.g., four or more bullet points per résumé item). Long strings of bulleted points tend be too dense to read quickly and easily. Always avoid repeating the same points using different phraseology. Above is the material from the previous résumé in paragraph formatting. The first item uses periods and the second semicolons. On an actual single résumé you would use either bullets or paragraphs, and, in paragraph formatting, either periods or semicolons.

One more format consideration is the overall length of your résumé. Paragraph formatting does allow you to include additional material on your résumé. If your résumé is one-and-a-half pages long with bullets, you might be able to reduce it to one sheet by converting the bulleted text to paragraphs, removing a few less significant items, and eliminating partial lines where only one or two words carry over to the next line. Similarly, you should be able to compress close to three pages of bulleted material into two pages of pithy paragraphs.

Just remember that paragraphs are more difficult to read quickly. If you choose to use paragraphs, keep them succinct. Resist the temptation to add less relevant material to paragraphs just because you have space left on a page. If you need to eliminate excess space on the bottom of a résumé page, try increasing page margins just a bit or expanding the spacing between main categories by a half or full line. You can also change category font size (e.g., from 14- to 15-point) or slightly increase the font size for your name.

Expert Advice

Focus on the Basics

"When it comes to the content of your résumé, a few key rules are: Keep it simple, keep it short, and keep it specific."

Brian Graham, *Get Hired Fast*

Edit, Edit, Edit

The quickest way to sabotage your chances of getting an interview is to submit a sloppily written or poorly formatted résumé. The care (or lack of care) you use to write and format your résumé reflects on your personal traits. Are you a messy person, as evidenced by margins that don't line up or by irregular spaces between résumé lines? Are you hasty, as reflected in the improper use of particular words? Even a few surface errors in a résumé can sink your interview chances by reflecting poorly on you. I've read error-riddled résumés from people applying for professorial jobs in communication! Incredibly, I've even seen them submitted by communication professors, including those who claim to teach writing.

Once you think you've finished polishing your résumé, read it over again, carefully. Then read it over still again. Then ask a few dependable friends to review it. Follow up by requesting that a parent, grandparent, or adult child proof it. Then get your pet bird to react to your résumé by putting a copy on the bottom of the cage. If the cutie offers any special "messages" on your résumé, you know you've got some work to do! Since any bird will gladly drop a bomb on your fresh prose, you'll get the message: Check it again!

Appendix F addresses many common grammatical hazards, but here are a few categories to keep in mind:

Expert Advice 📖

Small-Company Résumés

"Tone, grammar, and spelling are just as important for a résumé submitted to small companies. Work experience should be the first section of the résumé."

Nelda Spinks and Barron Wells, "Are Preferences of Small Companies Likely to Agree with Those of Large Corporations Concerning Résumés and Application Letter," *Bulletin of the Association for Business Communication*

- Spelling errors (Don't rely on your software spell-checker! Frequent errors include "its" vs. "it's," "their" vs. "there" and "they're," "principal" vs. "principle," and "a lot" vs. "alot"—the latter is not a word.)

- Commas everywhere or nowhere, regardless of proper usage

- Periods at the end of some phrases, even if they're not complete sentences. (Your options are to use (1) periods at the end of *every* bulleted line, (2), periods only for those of the bulleted lines that form complete sentences, or (3) no periods whatsoever.)

📖 *Expert Advice*

E-mail Your Résumé to Yourself

"If a potential employer wants you to put your résumé into the body of an email for submission (not as an attachment), first send the email to yourself to make sure that the formatting is proper. If not, make necessary changes and send yourself another test email."

Scott Bennett, *The Elements of Résumé Style: Essential Rules and Eye-Opening Advice for Writing Résumés and Cover Letters that Work*

■ Excessively long sentences or phrases (Short, direct language is best.)

■ Uppercase letters for all school subjects (Only actual languages, such as "English" and "Spanish," are capitalized; college majors and careers, such as sociology, engineering, religion, and accounting, are not.)

Semicolons are helpful punctuation marks; they tie together two related sentences to make one overall point. Dashes can serve a similar purpose—like this—if you need to insert a bit of related but parenthetical information into a sentence. Such dashes are meant to set off material you might otherwise introduce with "i.e." ("that is"). Note that such parenthetical dashes are longer than hyphens. They are typically located under "Symbols" under the "Insert" menu (if you're working in Microsoft Word®, check "Special Characters" under "More Symbols"). The longer em-dash is used as indicated above, while the somewhat shorter en-dash (–) serves to indicate a range, as, for example, between dates.

Once again, apart from grammar and layout hazards, the primary rule is consistency. For example, it isn't critical whether your lists include commas after every item except the last one ("red, white, and blue"; this last, optional comma is called a serial comma) or for all except the last two items ("red, white and blue"). Individual professional copyeditors do prefer various styles. But résumés aren't held to quite the same standard of grammatical precision. Just use acceptable grammar consistently.

Because copyediting is essential in résumé writing, never trust your own eyes. Run your résumé by others who are persnickety about grammar, style, and word choice. *Persnickety* is one of those great words that sound like what they mean—but don't use it on a résumé except perhaps to describe a former super-visor (just kidding!).

Make It Scannable

Most résumés should be *scannable*—i.e., composed in a format and style that will allow people to scan the document into a computer file, convert the resulting images to text, and then store the text in a search-able database of applicants. As a general rule, if someone can read your résumé quickly for the highlights, it will prob-ably be computer-scannable, too. But not always.

Dr. Q's tip

If your résumé is likely to be scanned by larger or online organizations, be sure you have included the "keywords" most frequently used in your field to describe important skills, knowledge, and traits—including technological skills and equipment. As mentioned earlier, consult want ads or with professionals in the field to find out what those might be. Correct grammar is an inadequate substitute for using career-specific language; you need both.

Larger for-profit and nonprofit organi-zations, along with most online job clear-inghouses and résumé-posting websites, employ special scanning technologies to convert résumés into text-based computer files. Think of this as the opposite of typing a résumé and printing it; these organizations scan image files and paper résumés and convert them back into word-searchable text documents.

Unfortunately, text-recognition scanning software cannot always convert visually fancy documents into readable text. Scanning soft-ware works best with simple, text-extensive résumés using standard fonts (e.g., Arial and Times New Roman), minimal graphics (e.g., bul-lets), adequate margins, and reasonably sized text (e.g., 11–12 point for the body and 13–14 point for your name). Generally speaking, such software works well with bold, underlined, italicized, and uppercase text but fails to accurately scan and store nonstandard fonts, clip art, text boxes (with visible borders), and other graphics, including atypical bullet symbols.

This is not a significant issue in artistic careers, where graphically intense résumés are common and where the printing of résumés on special, high-quality, colored paper is seen as an advantage for market-ing one's own creative skills. In the banking and financial arena, how-ever, the opposite is true: Résumés should be nearly all text (except for bullets) and should be printed on plain, bonded paper in white or conservative colors such as light gray, beige, or cream. Résumés printed on regular white copy paper seem "cheap", can easily get lost on a busy employer's cluttered desk, and are more prone to being misfiled with non-résumé material. Try 24lb. bonded stock.

In short, a layout and design with a few horizontal lines and standard bullets, printed in a standard font on light gray or beige paper, is most appropriate and well within the requirements for good readability and scanability. Think neatness, not cleverness. Just as you wouldn't want to dress too informally or too formally for an interview, present yourself appropriately in the "look" of your résumé.

Sometimes an employer will ask you to submit your résumé as an e-mail attachment. The employer might even specify a file format, such as Microsoft Word® or PDF. In such instances, keep in mind that the recipient might not be using the same version of software that you used to create the résumé file. The safest bet is to save your file in the second-most-recent version of the software if a brand-new version has already been released. Unless asked to do so, don't send multiple versions; the more choices you provide, the more work or confusion you create for recipients. If the employer doesn't request a specific file format, a PDF is usually the safest bet.

When submitting via e-mail attachment, include your cover letter in the same file format but *not* in the same document file as the résumé. Indicate in the e-mail subject line what you are sending and why: "Résumé and Cover Letter for Marketing Assistant Position, at Mr. Smith's Request." You may use clear abbreviations in order to reduce the overall length of your e-mail subject line: "Résumé/cover Mktg Asst via Mr. Smith." If you are sending the résumé and cover letter to an online e-mail such as a generic "application@e-mail," be especially careful to specify in the subject line any connection you've had with the organization to ensure that your submission will not be treated in the same manner as any unsolicited, anonymous submission. In any case, in addition to an attached cover letter, add a very short note in the e-mail to clarify what you are applying for and why:

Dear Ms. Jones (*or* "To Whom It May Concern"):

Attached are my résumé and cover letter for the Marketing Assistance position listed as #1740 on your website [or in a classified ad]. Mr. David Smith in your consumer affairs division encouraged me to apply after I met him at a recent career day.

Sincerely,
Your Name Here

Conclusion

The only truly effective résumés are fine-tuned résumés. Remember that a résumé is a presentation of who you are and what you offer prospective employers. Every résumé you submit needs to be carefully written, perfectly edited, and cleanly formatted. You don't want to boast, but you don't want to undersell yourself, either. Use precise action verbs. Say what you mean. Mean what you say.

What to Do Now

Fine-tune your sample résumés in line with the advice offered in this chapter. Tweak every résumé to fit a particular position. Also ensure that your cover letters (more on these in the next chapter) are similarly aimed at specific readers. If you're uncertain about using a summary statement rather than an objective statement, check with one or two professionals in the field. Along the way, be sure to save digital and/or printed copies of each fine-tuned résumé and cover letter; these copies will help you to quickly prepare later résumés and cover letters for similar career-launching positions.

Add References and Cover Letters

In this chapter you'll learn:

How to select and use references
How to write a persuasive cover letter

You've come a long way! You're close to completing an interview-producing résumé. But before you start celebrating, you'll want to offer appropriate thanks in order to maintain the best possible attitude. Give thanks for those who have offered advice and feedback along the way. If they've invested significant time, send them a quick thank-you note. Let them know you're heading down the final stretch. Never take such generosity for granted. Such advisers don't owe you anything. They're gifts.

Now you're ready to create some additional debts to kind-hearted people. You'll need some solid references who can attest to your character and professionalism. These folks can make or break your chances for an interview—and ultimately your job prospects as well. This chapter first offers advice about selecting and using references. Then it explains how to compose an effective cover letter that will please your potential employers and references alike.

Identify Your References

There's a saying that goes like this: "All references are good references." Everybody selects as references persons who are likely to give them positive evaluations. And every reference wants to give a positive assessment. Rarely will a personal or professional reference write a negative letter. After all, would you or any other career seeker ask someone to write a reference letter unless you knew it would be positive? Why would a prospective reference desire to hurt your career opportunities—unless you had done something horrible for which you had never apologized or otherwise mended your relationship with them? But remember this: It's far easier for a reference to offer generically positive comments about you to a potential new employer than it is for him or her to offer concrete, outstanding comments. In the back of the mind of every reference writer is the fact that they don't know you extremely well and that they don't want to testify to your greatness unless they can be certain you truly are great. Their credibility is at stake.

So the real issue for you goes beyond securing a few positive references in the form of letters or telephone conversations with potential employers. Anyone can do that. You need to do better. You need the right type of person providing the right kind of positive reference on your behalf. So consider these two factors: (1) what the job title, position, or organizational background of a specific reference suggests to a potential employer, and (2) when and how to provide specific positive references, including whether or not to list references on your résumé or to give them to possible employers later on in the job-search process. I'll tackle these two factors in order.

The Status of References

If you have numerous possibilities for references, select persons who offer the most prestige and credibility on the basis of their name, title, or organizational affiliation. For instance, a manager is better than an assistant manager. Actual professors carry more reference clout than do instructors or adjunct (part-time) teaching staff. Directors and heads of departments convey greater weight than do administrative assistants. A reference from a well-known national organization will give your résumé more punch than one from a relatively unknown, local company. A high-profile individual is a better reference than a low-profile person. No one has reference options that can maximize all of these categories. The secret is making sure you have the best possible kinds of references for a particular application. You might ask four or five people to serve as references for you, but even if they all agree you won't use every one of them for every application. Ordinarily the best three are sufficient.

Just be sure that every reference knows you well enough to be able to speak personally and concretely (citing specific examples) on your behalf. They have to be willing and able to write a personalized letter (or provide a phone reference) on your behalf and to provide it in a timely fashion upon request. It's often the case that the better known and more respected the person, the harder it is to contact them and actually get them to write a personalized reference letter or to provide an oral reference on the telephone. Some busy professionals who receive reams of requests for references resort to pre-written template letters, slightly changing the language for each letter. Others fail to perform the task even after they have agreed orally to do so. More on this issue below. Potentially positive references are not always dependable ones.

Even if you're married to the president of the company, don't use your relatives as references, since your potential employer understands that they will probably say good things about you no matter what. Besides, if a spouse or sibling gives you a less-than-spectacular reference, you've probably got a greater problem than the need to launch a career! If an application or job description requires a "character" or "personal" reference, use a mature adult who has known you for at least a couple of years and preferably holds a notable public position, such as a member of the clergy, a civic leader, or a current or recent professor. You can use a supervisor at a volunteer agency, too. Other options might include next-door neighbors, apartment mates, and coworkers who are not your supervisor. Never use significant others even if you assume the potential employer won't make the relational connection.

Making References Available

Unless a specific employer requests references up front, there is no special benefit and at least one drawback to listing them by name on your résumé. References are largely for (1) verifying the facts in your résumé and (2) ensuring that your personal character and work experience are positive. So references are generally contacted during the interviewing

☀ *Dr. Q's tip*

Including a term such as "references available upon request" on your résumé is usually a waste of precious résumé space. Would you ever not make them available?

process, not at the beginning stages of an application.

Moreover, adding specific references to your résumé takes up valuable real estate within those one or two pages you will need to tell your story as persuasively as possible. Of course, if a want ad requires or an employer requests references along with your résumé, you should provide complete contact information for every reference. But you can do this on a supplemental sheet (preferred); you don't have to list them on your résumé itself. As with all supplemental materials, include your name and contact information on the extra sheet and use the same color and weight of paper you use for your actual résumé and cover letter. Don't add references to the back of your résumé. Too often, employers will fail to see them or will forget to copy the back side when they distribute paper copies internally to colleagues.

In any case, be ready to move quickly when the request for references arrives. Get permission up front from supervisors or teachers (if you're still in school or if you're a recent graduate), along with one or two personal references, just in case. Give these references a copy of your résumé and cover letter so they know what you're up to. The better informed they are, the better they can serve you with a personalized, concrete reference. Broad, generalized references (e.g., "So and so is a good person and a fine worker.") never impress employers as much as concrete comments about your specific skills, knowledge, and traits.

If you really want to impress your references, as well as to serve them admirably, give them an additional couple of pages of information you have summarized from your Masterlist. This information might include lists of some of your skills, knowledge, and traits, along with a summary of some of your accomplishments, including those not included in your résumé. As much as possible, explain what you have done that exemplifies your specific skills, knowledge, and traits.

In the supplemental material you provide for each work reference, indicate both the work you did with them and any activities you undertook with him or her beyond your work. Never be satisfied with reminding references in general terms about your work with them. Offer them a broader view of the scope of your life story, too. Why? Because you can impress a reference just as much as you can impress a potential employer. The more excited your references are about your career candidacy, the more enthusiastic they will be to compose letters or engage in phone conversations on your behalf.

Be sure to clarify in your supplemental materials which of your completed and current activities involved a specific reference. One great way to accomplish this is to use asterisks to denote those specific activities a particular reference can address personally. Then put an asterisk (*) at the top or bottom of the supplemental Masterlist page(s) to indicate that:

*Items with asterisks relate directly to my activities with you and/or your organization.

Finally, provide in your supplemental material for each reference a paragraph summary of your specific connection to her or him—where and how you met, as well as your position when you worked or volunteered with them. This gives your reference a quick means to recall your activities more fully. The easier you make it for references (without drafting the letter for them), the better. If your references include current or former teachers, you should list the classes you took with them, the grades you received, and any special projects or papers you completed in those classes. If you didn't do as well in the course as you would have liked, let them know why (assuming you had personal issues at the time—such as working 40 hours weekly while a full-time student). If your references include former work supervisors, list the tasks and projects you completed under their guidance. Once again, assist your busy references by providing concrete, personal information. Don't be surprised if they borrow much of your language for their actual letter. Just don't tell them what to say.

What if one of your best references agrees to write only one non-confidential letter on your behalf? In other words, what if she or he is unwilling to write letters fine-tuned for specific jobs, organizations, and recipients? While this reluctance is no longer common, it can occur in at least three specific situations: (1) when large university classes make it difficult for professors to get to know their students

Dr. Q's tip

If you're applying for a position that requires you to submit a "waiver of access rights" form, always sign it positively and include it with your résumé and any other requested materials. These waivers are used extensively for academic applications (such as for graduate school) and give you a chance to forego your right to see your references' letters. If you don't sign the waiver, both the graduate school and your reference writers will know that you will be able to read what the references say about you. Generally speaking, this will create the impression that you have something to hide and that you might not trust your own references.

well, (2) when an employer or nonprofit supervisor is responsible for the efforts of someone under their authority but haven't gotten to know that person particularly well, and (3) when someone is leaving an organization (voluntarily or involuntarily) and the supervisor is willing to write only a generic letter of reference attesting to the employee's character and/or broad skills and knowledge.

In the past, references would frequently give these nonconfidential letters to job seekers to copy and show directly to potential employers. Often job-seekers' résumés were part of a portfolio that included copies of such reference letters and related documents, such as employee evaluations, thank-you letters from satisfied customers or clients, and copies of nonconfidential materials the seeker completed on the job (e.g., reports, memoranda, letters, position papers, proposals, and findings). Portfolios are still preferred in some fields and required in a few, but nonconfidential letters of reference are rarely used today. Most employers nowadays require that confidential letters be sent directly from the reference-letter writer to the potential employer or filled out and submitted online. Ironically, even these letters can be very general, because the writers may fear being sued if their negative comments are eventually shared with an applicant.

Many organizations today conduct confidential phone interviews of references rather than using letters. They want to know the truth about you, often without a paper trail. They also hope to speed up the hiring process and avoid litigation for discrimination or other legal issues. Former employees and students who provide me with their information sheets along with copies of their résumés are more likely to receive a positively persuasive, concrete telephone reference because

I can refer to specifics on the page, even while conversing with prospective employers.

When you are asked for references, always provide employers with the following information about each one:

- The reference's complete, professional name
- The reference's current title or position, including titles to be used in addressing that person (e.g., Dr., Ms., Rev., President)
- The reference's current employer
- The title or position of the person at the time you worked with them, if different
- The reference's organizational title and affiliation when you worked with them (Indicate "formerly with" in parentheses.)
- The reference's current work telephone number, including any office extension, unless it's a personal reference (Then provide cell and/or home phone numbers, as well as office information.)
- The reference's current office address
- The reference's current office fax number
- The reference's current work e-mail address

A listing of references on a sheet of paper supplemental to your résumé should read something like this, with the same font and layout style as your résumé:

Bethany J. Biker
References

Ms. Yvonne R. Postman
Sales Manager
Sharp Photo Stores
1208 Clearbrooke Blvd.
Watkinsville, GA 99999
(777) 777-7777, ext. 123
(777) 777-7771 (fax)
person@permanentaddress.net

Some professions use a "credential file" for entry-level applications. Many colleges, for instance, require education students to compile an electronic or paper file that includes everything from reference letters to writing samples. Then any hiring school can simply request a student's complete file; the student doesn't have to worry about asking references to send letter after letter to different schools, and schools don't have to organize all of the incoming letters for each applicant.

Compiling a credential file is a valuable experience because it helps college students to identify quality references and to evaluate their own skills. Unfortunately, the included reference letters won't be tweaked for a specific position or for a particular organization. If the application process for a position requires a credential file, then by all means explain in your résumé how to access the information. Otherwise, leave it out. If you're applying for a particularly important position, you can always request that the potential employer permit you to solicit fresh letters sent directly from references to the employer. Just don't push the matter, or it might seem to the employer that you are trying to avoid letting him or her see your file because it potentially includes negative material.

It's appropriate to send your references a thank-you note. Even if you don't secure the position, you should express your appreciation for their help. If you *do* get the job, it's critical to thank them personally for their part in the process. They'll be pleased to know you've been successful. Such letters always make my day; they put a song in my heart. I get to celebrate with friends and colleagues, as well as with the person for whom I wrote the letter.

Write Persuasive Cover Letters

It's likely that you'll have to submit résumés to people who have not specifically requested them from you. For instance,

📖 *Expert Advice*

Fine-Tune Each Résumé and Cover Letter

"Even if your résumé is superbly written and designed, you'll receive more positive responses if the résumé and the cover letter are finely tuned for each position and organization."

Scott Bennett, *The Elements of Résumé Style: Essential Rules and Eye-Opening Advice for Writing Résumés and Cover Letters That Work* you might post a résumé on a career website, send a résumé in response to a classified newspaper ad, or submit a résumé to an organization listed at your school's employment office. In these cases, you'll want to send a one-page cover letter along with the résumé. The cover letter is critically important because potential employers know that you will have to write one separately for each possible position. They want to see how well you can make your case with the cover letter, apart from your résumé. Résumés can be more or less standardized for a type of position, whereas effective cover letters are invariably organization specific, as well as position focused.

Every good cover letter needs to include the following, usually in this order:

1. A clear statement regarding the particular job for which you are applying—even the specific title of the position and/or the job number, as stated in the job listing

2. An indication of where you heard about the position (such as from an advertisement or through a friend or an employee of the organization—the latter can be especially helpful for you and for them, but don't refer to insiders who might provide anything less than a sterling recommendation)

3. A statement about why you are interested in the position and the organization (maybe you're moving to that area or have heard great things about the organization through other employees)

Expert Advice 📖

Cover Your Pitch

Cover letters are meant to be persuasive, not just factual. "A cover letter is a sales presentation in disguise."

Ford R. Myers, *Get the Job You Want, Even When No One's Hiring*

Expert Advice 📖

Cover the Essentials

"Except in rare circumstances, a cover letter should fit on one page, be crisp and punchy, and demonstrate that you're familiar with the organization you're applying to."

Michael E. Hattersly, "Writing the Perfect Cover Letter: Strategies for Nailing Your Dream Job," *Harvard Management Communication Letter*

4. An explanation as to why you think you are qualified for this position

5. An indication that you know something significant about the organization and are not just mass-mailing résumés and cover letters for all positions that look potentially interesting to you

Also, be sure to address the letter to the specific person and department provided in the information you have received and verified. Just as with résumés, any cover letter typos, grammatical mistakes, or factual errors are unacceptable. Get others to proof your letter. Write it clearly and succinctly. Cover letters sometimes persuade, but they shouldn't boast or make desperate claims. ("You're my last hope. If you don't hire me, I won't be able to pay my rent.") Appendix G includes sample résumés with accompanying cover letters, so you can see how the two work together.

Cover letters sometimes seem frivolous. Isn't your cover letter just a rehash of your résumé? No. Cover letters give employers a chance to see whether you're really serious about *them*. They also give *you* an opportunity to explain briefly why you're the right person, both for the organization and for the position. Therefore, use your cover letters to interest employers in you and in your résumé. A cover letter is the closest you'll get to a free advertisement for your services. It affords you a legitimate opportunity to put a positive spin on your résumé.

Here's the really good news about composing effective cover letters: If you wrote your résumé according to the principles in this book, you've already written much of your letter. Why? Because a great cover letter applies the basic material in your résumé to the specific job and organization. It explains why you're interested in the position and why you believe you're qualified, based on the documentation you provide in your résumé. Your summary statement, in particular, should be the basis for your persuasive cover letter.

The more you practice fine-tuning your résumés and composing persuasive but honest cover letters, the less time and aggravation you'll experience in the future. For one thing, you can use a lot of your existing material, including your Masterlist. For another, you'll come to know how to fine-tune your material quickly for different audiences. Finally, you'll have discovered which references will provide solid feedback in a timely manner. Remember to keep both digital and paper copies of all of your cover letters, résumés, and Masterlists. I encourage you to update the computer file name every time you create a new version of any of these three documents (i.e., do a "save as" and re-date the file name).

You'll still have to take the time to make sure each cover letter is appropriate for the specific organization and position for which you're applying. Don't just use a standardized cover letter that fails to show why you're interested in a specific job and a particular organization. Don't be surprised if you get interviews for positions you're really not qualified to hold; good cover letters demonstrate how serious you are about an organization. Sometimes career-related enthusiasm, coupled with the use of professional language, generates employer interest in considering an applicant for other positions.

Conclusion

References and cover letters are critically important for career seekers. Just today I attended a search committee meeting for reviewing the first round of applicants for a position. We discussed the

Expert Advice 📖

Stay Warm-Hearted

"Avoid two emotional extremes in electronically submitted cover letters: (1) bland, disinterested prose, and (2), overly emotional enthusiasm. Ensure that your cover letter communicates your interest and enthusiasm without either extreme."

Sam H. DeKay, "Expressing Emotion in Electronic Job Cover Letters," *Business Communication Quarterly* résumés, but we also discussed the required lists of applicant references. Questions went like this:

- Who knows any of these references?
- Do these look like solid references?
- Why are female references referred to as "Mrs." rather than "Ms.?"
- Shouldn't there be character as well as professional references?

I saw once again that the references themselves—let alone their letters—can make or break applicants' chances. Employers interpret the value of specific references even before they have contacted any of them specifically. The question of whether to use "Mrs." or "Ms." for a reference is easily solved by not using either one. But employers' perceptions of such things as references' job titles and organizational affiliations are somewhat subjective. Again, be sure to ask a couple people in the field to review your résumé and references before you send them to any potential employer. Ask them how they perceive your references. Then edit accordingly.

At the same meeting we reviewed cover letters, hoping to better understand some of the "raw" material on the résumés. This time the questions went like this:

- Why is this person applying for this job?
- Does the cover letter explain what the applicant has been doing for the last four years (the résumé didn't)?
- Wow, this is a great cover letter, isn't it?
- I can't believe we didn't receive a cover letter with this résumé. Are you sure we didn't somehow misplace it (we didn't)?

On and on go such meetings, as search committees seek to better understand applicants' motivations, experience, and accomplishments. Taken together, cover letters, résumés, and even lists of references provide a profile of each applicant. So work wisely on all three, giving thanks as you complete tasks and recruit supportive reference persons to speak on your behalf.

What to Do Now

Once you've finished a résumé and an accompanying cover letter, be sure to ask some friends and coworkers to review them. Ask for honest, critical advice. Try giving them a high-quality red pen they can use to write comments on your documents. Encourage them to get back at all their nitpicky teachers by taking out their literary frustrations on you. Invite them to keep the pen, too! Then start contacting potential reference persons, sending them copies of your perfectly polished prose.

Go with the Flow

In this chapter you'll learn:

What not to worry about on your résumé
How to get and use feedback on your résumé
Special ways to circulate—and not to circulate—your résumé

Searching for job openings, developing a Masterlist, writing and revising résumés, filling out applications, sending out résumés, furnishing references, asking references to write letters and to be available for phone calls—all of this work is stressful. So as you take the final steps of résumé writing, it's good to know what's worth worrying about and what's not worth losing any sleep over. It's also helpful to continue getting feedback on your résumé so you can tweak it to near perfection. Finally, you should start circulating your résumé wisely. This chapter covers all of these topics, providing the insights you'll need in order to remain coolly self-confident as potential employers start calling you to schedule interviews.

Don't Sweat It

An ancient prayer asks for strength to do what we need to do, as well as to accept whatever we cannot change. This is good advice for career-seeking college students, too. Not just prayer, but casting off anxiety. No matter how much effort you've put into résumé writing, you can't control the outcome. Worrying won't help. It's interesting to note that Jesus' most frequent words of advice were "Fear not."

Which task is more difficult for you, beginning something new or leaving something alone? For many of us, trusting our destiny is insufficient; we want to control the outcomes. We usually don't like telling other people what to do—just as we don't appreciate others telling us what to do. In either case, a controlling attitude creates conflicts and stress. So we're stuck in the middle. We'd like to influence potential employers without coming on too strongly. It's like dating someone we really like, all the while worrying that our excessive enthusiasm could scare them away.

There's nothing wrong with wanting job hunting to go your own way. But fretting doesn't help your cause. Neither does pushiness. Even in job searching we can be our own worst enemies.

When it comes to résumé writing, being a control freak can be an undesirable trait. Résumés are just one factor in a complicated world of hirings and firings, interviews and rejection letters, internal politics, economic fluctuations, good news and bad news—or no news at all. You'll try to imagine how employers will respond to your résumés and cover letters. How will you fare against other applicants? You'll even anticipate one or another outcome, replaying various scenarios in your mind. I've known students who've had nightmares about the whole job-search process. For some of them, the worst part is actually getting interview requests, because then they agonize about having to go to the interviews and fret about what they can say without making fools of themselves. So while they want their résumé and cover letter to elicit interview requests, they're apprehensive about actually getting any interviews. Such is human nature.

Then there's the second-guessing: Why didn't you emphasize one skill more than another one on your résumé? Were you too humble or excessively assertive in your cover letter? What can you do better next time around, even though you haven't yet gotten a response to your current submission? All of this nonproductive worrying and second-guessing leads to anxious thoughts and restless nights.

If you allow anxiety to get the better of you, you'll tend to become impatient and even critical when you don't hear back quickly from employers. You'll get down on these prospective employers and on yourself. And in the process you'll become less effective in résumé writing and interviewing. Your attitude can spiral into cynical hopelessness.

As I mentioned, this experience is similar to dating anxieties. I have no desire to go back to high school and deal with the uncertainties and angst of dating. I think that, if I had it to do over again, I would prefer to jump from about 12 to 21 years of age. Or from my first part-time job to my first promising professional career position. For me, marriage is terrific but dating was often more stressful than fun. Here's a somewhat serious prayer for college students: "God, please grant me a great job without the stress of finding and getting it."

This is why it's healthy to consider with regard to a résumé what is worth fretting about (typos!) and what's not worth losing sleep over (why you've never heard back from a potential employer). "Romancing" employers with your love letters (résumés and cover letters) is never stress free, but the process can be less anxiety inducing if you maintain the kind of positive attitude I discussed in Chapter 1. The following considerations probably aren't worth any worry equity when it comes to job applications in general and résumé writing in particular:

You've got the wrong degree for the job—as though everything you've done in life and all of your personal character traits are necessarily less important than the specific degree you may have earned: B.S., B.A., B.F.A., etc. Some students hold stereotypes about specific college majors (e.g. biology majors = smart; engineering majors = geeky; communications majors = lazy). Few employers hold such stereotypes. It's true that applicants must in some cases hold particular degrees for graduate school or for particular jobs. Fields like education, accounting, and social work emphasize proper academic credentials. For most entry-level jobs positions, however, general experience, personal character, and transferable skills are more significant to employers.

Even two or three years down your career path, chances are that few potential employers will ever ask about your major at the "U." They'll be more interested in whether or not you earned a degree than in the degree itself. They'll care more about your work history than about your academic activities. Employers might continue to be impressed with the school you attended if it's a high-profile academic institution or if they attended and appreciated their own education at the same college. Nevertheless, in most careers post-college experience rapidly trumps educational degrees and academic pedigrees. College sometimes functions more as a rite of passage or a union card than as a solid career development program. I say this as a 35-year professor who visits many university campuses and mentors scores of former students.

Suppose you've got an elementary education degree in a tight local job market in terms of where you want to live. Suppose, too, that you'd strongly prefer not to relocate where the prospects are better. What can you do? Why not apply for related non-education positions even as you continue searching for a teaching opportunity? The fact that you're personally well rounded and dedicated will matter for other careers, too. So will your educational training. You might end up working for a while in a preschool job or in a human relations office, orienting new employees.

What if you're interested in teaching but don't have an education degree? Suppose you live in a state or province with a shortage of elementary educators and in which the government doesn't require teaching credentials, let alone an education degree. Some governments do provide a means for college graduates without education degrees to become full-time, tenure-earning teachers, usually under the mentorship of a master teacher. Applicants for these kinds of teaching positions rarely hold education degrees.

The lesson is to avoid limiting your career search just because you have or have not earned a particular degree. Let potential employers decide whether or not you're qualified based on your overall résumé, not just on your academic pedigree. You never know what job you might land and what career you'll end up in.

You've got the wrong kinds of experience—as though you've messed up everything in your life and there's no turning back, no chance to redeem yourself in the eyes of hypercritical employers who would love to reject your flimsy application, laughable résumé, and hollow cover letter. Do you really believe that your past determines your future?

That you can't improve your life? That personal careers either ascend or descend without bumps and zigzags?

Life is all about change. Life is learning, growing, and discovering more about yourself and others. Fits and starts are the norm, not the exception. Every day thousands of people redirect their career paths, even though they may already be experiencing success in one particular field. Sometimes they're bored, unfulfilled, or stressed out. In other instances they discover a line of work that seems more interesting, holds greater promise for personal advancement, or will help them to better balance work, play, and family.

If you focus on your basic, transferable skills, knowledge, and traits, you'll discover multiple career paths that may be open to you. As I mentioned earlier, skilled teachers don't have to instruct just classroom students. They can transfer their skills to workplace education, such as teaching new employees about company policies or instructing them on customer relations and group dynamics. Business persons can shift to the nonprofit sector, working for religious organizations, governmental agencies, or non-governmental organizations. Chemists can become pharmaceutical representatives. Specific jobs come and go. Careers evolve. Life experience is always teaching us job-transferable, career-preparing skills, knowledge, and traits.

Life itself is experience, an educational journey. Most skills can be picked up along the way. After all, some employers actually prefer to hire new career seekers with less profession-specific experience. They believe that quality people are trainable investments in their organization's future. So be sure to emphasize the key items from your Masterlist, rather than fretting about every little detail of how you can sell yourself for a specific job for which you seem to lack experience. Don't be naively optimistic, as though you'll invariably

Expert Advice 📖

Include Extracurricular Activities

"Be sure to add to your résumé those academic and extracurricular activities that document your experience in basic skills such as *teamwork* and *leadership*. Otherwise recruiters may not realize the extent to which your particular coursework included such skills."

Terri Feldman Barr and Kevin M. McNeilly, "The Value of Students' Classroom Experience in the Eyes of the Recruiter: Information, Implications, and Recommendations for Marketing," *Journal of Marketing Education* be the best person for any position. Don't fire off résumés for high-demand jobs for which you don't have a lick of related experience and don't meet any of the posted job requirements. Yet avoid self-defeating pessimism, too, as though you don't have a chance at any career-opening job on the planet.

You feel guilty using nonpaid experience on your résumé—as though laboring for free is less valuable than laboring for money. Actually, one could make the opposite case—that amateur activities (an "amateur" is literally someone who does something for the "love" of it) are more telling than what employees do when the payroll clock is running. Your ideal occupation is probably getting paid to do what you most like to do. Economic realities might make it unlikely that you'll be able to make a living doing only what you enjoy doing, but making yourself marketable makes a big difference no matter which careers you pursue. The idea of selling your abilities to others—of persuading others that you know and believe in yourself—is key to becoming a money-earning "amateur" in your line of work. Employers seek both talented and enthusiastic workers. In many cases skill isn't enough. Attitude is essential. Your attitudes are formed in and through your life experience, which is the foundation for your Masterlist and résumé.

You achieved less-than-spectacular college grades—as though grades are necessarily related to success, and as though everyone in your future will interrogate you about every last grade you've ever received. Chances are that people reviewing your résumé didn't always receive the greatest grades, either. If you flunked out of courses repeatedly, so that your résumé is half comprised of a list of schools that gave you the boot, you've got some explaining to do. The first question is why you stayed in school when you obviously lacked maturity at that point in your life.

On the other hand, maybe you've gained quite a bit of experience figuring

📖 *Expert Advice*

Dream *and* Act

What are you doing with your résumé? "You can want and hope and dream until your wishbone is worn out, and nothing will happen unless you act."

Nicholas Lore, *Now What?*

out how to talk your way back into school. You're an amateur PR agent who has spent hours successfully pitching your seemingly hopeless personal case to principals, deans, professors, and other educational gate-keepers. Or maybe you've been cobbling together numerous odd jobs to make ends meet, working outlandish hours, plugging away at life in a seesaw economy, wearing out your work shoes on sidewalks, all the while fine-tuning your résumé. Persistence might be one of your admirable traits!

Expert Advice 📖

Be Proactive

"Your job search will be more successful if you cultivate a proactive personality."

Douglas J. Brown, et. al., "Proactive Personality and the Successful Job Search: A Field Investigation with College Graduates," *Journal of Applied Psychology*

When I attended my ten-year high school reunion, I discovered that some of the top graduates had done poorly by society's standards. They were not all respected professionals in law, medicine, or business. I also noticed that some of the ostensibly "least-likely-to-succeed" students had prospered personally and financially. I reflected that I was in the latter category—a high school loser who had become a respected college professor. I had learned after high school, and even late in my own college student days, to work hard, learn from others' experience, and organize my career-related activities. My grades improved, but more importantly I became a dedicated, productive person interested in serving others rather than just in advancing my own career. I, too, discovered the value of a mature "B" student over an "A" student with an attitude problem.

In my three decades as a college teacher and life mentor for hundreds of former students, I've witnessed firsthand the imperfect correlation between academic achievement and life success. There are two tracks in lifelong learning: formal and informal education. Some people are able to shuttle back and forth, applying learning from one track to the other one and vice versa. Most of us learn primarily in one direction. For instance, we apply life lessons to careers; the business sections of bookstores are loaded with titles that make this point. In business more than in most other fields, it's acceptable and sometimes even admirable to become a self-taught success with or without an impressive educational record. Why? Because life experience is a kind of textbook for learning about relationships, careers, and just about anything else.

You don't have any good academic references—as though you never got to know any teachers well enough for them to speak on your behalf. Actually, this is a fairly common problem, especially for college students who attended large state universities, where some classes fill cavernous lecture halls and where many are taught by graduate assistants rather than professors. While a student, I once received a letter from my university that began, "Dear [social security number]." The first line read, "We have a personal interest in you." *Huh?*

So here's my professorial advice for college students, college dropouts, and college graduates alike who need a reference: Contact one of your favorite professors, who genuinely seemed like a nice person, who obviously cared about students' well-being, even if you never got to know her or him personally. Nine times out of ten this kind of helpful, student-focused teacher will be glad to assist you because your appreciation of them honors their work. Give him or her your prepared materials for references, as discussed above, so the professor can have some honest, straightforward background information on you. Also offer to answer any additional questions about yourself, including both your weaknesses and your strengths. Be humble and grateful. Soon you'll have some helpful references.

Expert Advice

Go After Interviews

Your attitude toward job searching is critically important. Your own active, intense job searching increases your chances of landing interviews. Moreover, job interviews predict job offers, and job offers predict employment status.

Alan M. Saks, "Multiple Predictors and Criteria of Job Search Success," *Journal of Vocational Behavior*

Circulate Your Résumé Strategically

Pat was a former student of mine who exhibited seemingly boundless energy, even five years after college. I received at least one e-mail from him weekly, usually a vigorously argued essay about a major news item. He loved to express articulate opinions about everything from politics to religion. Some of Pat's opinion pieces included his personal experiences as an employee for a security agency.

When Pat asked for permission to use my name as a reference for jobs in the financial industry, I was delighted to consent. I could imagine Pat spending hours and hours online, learning the ins and outs of all things monetary, just as he must have spent most evenings surfing the Web for news stories and data to support his weekly e-mail missives. I imagined Pat selling securities, being an independent insurance agent, or writing mortgages. Pat was a go-getter, energy in motion.

After more than a month went by with no e-mail from Pat and no requests either from employers or from Pat himself for references, I grew puzzled and even a bit concerned. Where was Pat? Maybe he had talked the government into appointing him as secretary of finance, I chuckled to myself. Soon the expected e-mail arrived—a tersely worded message indicating only that he had a new e-mail address, not from a new employer but from one of the largest free e-mail services. I couldn't help but reply to him with a quick question: "New job?"

"Nope," he responded later that night. "Spam. Lots of it. Job offers. Résumé-writing pitches. Résumé-posting offers. Sales positions. Posted my résumé online. Help!"

Oh, the joys of circulating a résumé in a high-tech world! Pat learned his lesson the hard way: Circulating a résumé should be strategic rather than numerical. Mass-marketing yourself by posting résumés across the Internet is a recipe for disaster. Do career seekers find jobs by mass-circulating résumés? Rarely. These hyped-up résumé recyclers end up being the targets of shrewd charlatans selling résumé-writing, résumé-distributing, résumé-posting, and résumé-designing services that are sometimes scams. Seekers also get inundated with pitches for questionable jobs, from work-at-home "money makers" to

Expert Advice 📖

Post Your Résumé Online?

Posting your résumé online is probably not worth your time. Why? When employers post their positions online, they "are immediately flooded with hundreds of résumés, many from people whose backgrounds are wildly inappropriate."

David H. Freedman, "The Monster Dilemma: Posting Jobs on the Web is Easy. It's Sifting through Hundreds of Resumés that's a Pain," *Inc. Magazine*

📖 *Expert Advice*

Apply Online to Large Companies

"77% of Fortune 500 companies prefer online submissions of application information and résumés—usually via the companies' own websites. Big companies are moving away from fax and paper submissions and from scanning paper and digital image files."

Nancy M. Schullery, Linda Ickes, and Stephen E. Schullery, "Employer Preferences for Résumés and Cover Letters," *Business Communication Quarterly*

commission-only sales positions, multi-level marketing gimmicks, and high-fee job "placement" services.

Pat had not only elicited a storm of e-mail pitches. Thanks to the online "robots" that collect Web-posted e-mail addresses and sell them to third parties, his references were similarly bombarded with junk e-mail about ways to make a fortune in a new career. I know. I was one of them, furiously deleting a daily dose of employment spam that was managing to leak through my e-mail filters.

In most professions there is no quick, safe, cheap way to circulate your résumé online to only the many organizations that have available positions fitting your skills, knowledge, and traits. The Internet is great for submitting résumés and cover letters to specific employers. The medium can also work well for posting résumés on password-protected, usually member-only websites for particular professional associations (like the "National Association of…") that represent respected professions and professionals. There are some major, legitimate résumé-posting, employer-supported websites that successfully match seekers with opportunities within specific, often technical, high-demand fields. But the most worthwhile online job sites serve primarily employers in fields in which the demand for employees outstrips the supply (e.g., nursing, engineering, accounting, and physical therapy).

The lesson for most career seekers is to circulate résumés strategically rather than willy-nilly. Here are some basic tips to avoid wasting your time and energy and to stay on the good side of your e-mail-saturated references:

- Post your résumé on one of the major job sites only if the service is free and has an "anonymous" feature so employers can't gain access to your private information (such as e-mail and address) without your permission.

- Concentrate on submitting résumés and cover letters to actual organizations via their own websites, on which specific openings are listed. This is more work than posting your material on a massive job clearinghouse website, but it demonstrates your initiative, as well as your interest in the specific organization.

- Never respond to e-mail from someone who claims to have "just the career-advancement opportunity" for you, even if they know your name. These are nearly all scams designed to lure you into paying for worthless services or to get you to reveal personal financial information, such as checking account or credit card numbers.

- If you apply for a federal government job online, you'll be asked to provide your Social Security information, but there is no other case in which you should have to provide your Social Security number or a scan of your driver's license for an initial, online application.

- Talk to friends, family, and neighbors about who they know in your fields of interest. Ask them whether you may mention their names in a cover letter that you would send with your résumé to only friends of friends. See appendix G for sample cover letters you can tweak for such person-to-person résumé networking.

- Ask friends in related fields or search online to determine which professional associations meet regularly in your area. Contact the local event organizer and inquire regarding the possibility of attending a meeting to find out more about the organization and its member services. Ask about official networking opportunities and any directories of e-mail mailing lists for local members that you may use to let members know who you are and what you have to offer.

- Schedule some local informational interviews, as described in chapter 3, to determine which professional associations are most active, when and where they meet, and the major employers in that field.

- Volunteer with local nonprofit agencies that have employees who do the kinds of work you hope to turn into a career. As you assist such organizations, you'll also discover more about the career and your area's movers and shakers. You'll even hear about organizational changes and openings.

- If you attended college, check with your alma mater to see what services it offers alums. Start with the alumni office and, if necessary, consider contacting the career development office directly. Find out whether there is an alumni network for helping alums connect by profession within a particular geographic area. Many alumni groups now provide this assistance on an opt-in basis so that only willing alums can be contacted for help by job-seeking alums.

Expert Advice

Resist the Hype about Online Résumé-Posting

"At one website with 30,000 posted résumés, only 15 employers even looked at the site over three months."

Richard N. Bolles, *What Color is Your Parachute?*

Among the craziest gimmicks for circulating résumés are fee-based services that essentially turn your résumé into spam and blast it to half a million or more "companies." This might at least momentarily seem like a good way to charge another $50 to your worn out credit card, but resist the urge. Take a deep breath. Think soberly about any résumé-routing scheme that seems too easy to be worthwhile. It is.

What about posting your résumé on your own website? Be careful here, too. It's a great idea to create your own, high-quality website as a kind of online portfolio. This is becoming increasingly popular and effective in the arts, communications, and business. But the value of online résumé and portfolio material is not based on chance website visits from potential employers. Successful online self-promotion needs to be linked to the traditional means of searching for jobs and circulating résumés. You'll still have to get your résumés and cover letters into the hands of individuals and organizations. Then, in both your cover letter and résumé, you can direct potential employers to your website, where you can provide more evidence of your life experience as it has prepared you for a career.

There are downsides to online résumé and portfolio websites, too. First, don't include particularly personal information that thieves might use to steal your identity. Second, your online résumé will have to be more generic than the specialized versions you send to specific people and organizations. Third, older versions of your online material will continue to reside in online search engines that index older Web content. One way of minimizing these problems is to keep your website as private as possible by resisting the urge to link to it from any other pages. Don't even give out the address to friends and family. Offer it only to potential employers. Between 60 percent and 80 percent of successful job searches involve a combination of

Expert Advice 📖

Compare Your Online Persona to Your Résumé

"Make sure to review the material that you post on your personal blog and social networking website (SNW) to see if it matches the personal traits in your résumé. Students whose SNWs are family- or professional-oriented are seen as more suitable for employment than those whose SNWs are alcohol-oriented."

Daniel Bohnert and William H. Ross, "The Influence of Social Networking Web Sites on the Evaluation of Job Candidates," *Cyberpsychology, Behavior, and Social Networking*

Dr. Q's tip 🔆

Career seeking is not mass-marketing. It's selective, strategic communication with focused résumé writing and cover-letter persuasion. Think selectively. Focus your energy.

If you try to communicate with everyone in general, you'll end up communicating with no one in particular. Moreover, you'll get depressed about the lack of personal responses.

📖 *Expert Advice*

Think Digital—Not Just Print

"Even at career fairs, representatives from larger companies are increasingly declining to accept printed résumés. Instead, representatives direct interested students to company websites to apply for positions and submit résumés."

Nancy M. Schullery, Linda Ickes, and Stephen E. Schullery, "Employer Preferences for Résumés and Cover Letters," *Business Communication Quarterly*

old-fashioned, local, in-person networking and in-print and online research about specific openings within particular organizations.

Create a Support Network

Hopping from one go-nowhere job to the next one while applying for career positions can be doubly stressful. But if you surround yourself with supportive friends you can avoid being swallowed up by stress. The demands of résumé writing, cover-letter composing, and career hunting are shared by many people, even in good economic times. You don't have to face the uncertain future on your own. Don't even try to do so. Instead, band together with other positive-minded career seekers and support one another. Meanwhile, avoid inviting cynics and naysayers into your group. They can turn your support group into a gaggle of job-seeking worrywarts.

Form a group of career seekers to have fun together and to remain hopeful, even as you struggle to find a fitting career or a fine employer. Work hard, but then relax. Play games. Watch comedies. Ride bikes or horses or motorcycles. Jog together if you're knee pumpers. Strive to do it all with people you enjoy. They know you, including your real value as a distinct, one-of-a-kind human being. That recognition will keep you going as you travel the long, bumpy road from résumé writing to first, second, and perhaps even third or fourth careers. As I tell my college students, I'm still trying to figure out what I'm going to be when I grow up. I teach. I write. I mentor. I consult. I "bird" (as in "birdwatching"). I have fun even if some days I don't know exactly how to describe my so-called career.

Conclusion

By now you know the biggest secret of this book: A great résumé is all about life, not just work. Writing an effective résumé is about learning how to pursue a great life, a well-rounded life, a life that accepts the inevitable ups and downs but remains optimistic and forward leaning in spite of the challenges. In the beginning of this book I called you to be courageous, not just practical. I also asked you to be a bit vulnerable, even while fully clothed.

So relax! Get a life, and then enjoy it! If you're up-tight, you won't impress others in an interview. Worrying won't help. What will? Writing employer-focused résumés and cover letters and sending them out strategically.

For all of the work involved in composing a résumé, don't let it consume you. Cultivate friendships along the way, especially friendships with other career seekers. Take a few risks, but not outrageous ones. Polish your résumé language and design your résumé pages with all the energy of squirrels scurrying around yards, hiding nuts, and building up storehouses of sustenance for tough weather ahead. But be sure to celebrate along the way as you and your career-seeking friends complete each step, from Masterlists to careers.

Not long ago I received an e-mail from Cathy, a former student who was depressed about being unable to find a decent job. Cathy had done everything right, including writing a solid résumé that had landed her a terrific internship. But the internship was nearly over, and she had no future job prospects. Half the places at which Cathy had applied hadn't even responded to her carefully crafted cover letters. I wanted to cry with her. We live in emotionally trying times for many college students who will make wonderful employees but have few chances to prove themselves and make the necessary career inroads.

Soon Cathy sent me a follow-up e-mail brimming with so much excitement that it lacked standard punctuation. No, she hadn't received a single job offer from any of the applications. She hadn't even gotten an interview. As the all-lowercase e-mail peppered with exclamation marks explained, Cathy's intern supervisor had decided to make a case to his boss to hire her. And he had succeeded. Why? Because she had proven herself to be a dependable, teachable, and gifted person. Again, I wanted to cry, but this time with tears of joy.

Life experience is the key to writing a great résumé because it's the key to living wisely and well. Experience is the way we learn—or at least the way we *should* learn. We humans have to live in order to learn—and learn in order to live. We have to grow into careers. Writing a résumé based on life experience is one way to prepare yourself for life, for a career. Not just for a job.

As you approach the employment market, use every ounce of experience you have—all of the resources at your disposal. If you're a religious person, by all means pray for success. If you have two kinds of friends—the grumpy ones and the thankful ones—hang out with the latter group as you go through résumé writing and career seeking. Don't allow yourself to become critical of others along the way, including those who fail to respond to your résumés and cover letters, those who come across in interviews as disinterested or arrogant, and those who don't bother to respond to your request for a reference. I've seen repeatedly that college students' poor attitudes toward others can adversely affect their self-images and hurt their chances. We have to believe in ourselves. We need to remind ourselves that we have value as individual persons. That's basic. It's the right foundation on which to build.

I've also learned that interviews and jobs are often given to particular people for odd reasons. Sometimes seekers know the right people. They happen to be in the right place at the right time. One of my former students happened to see a sign on an office building, wondered what exactly the company did, went inside to inquire, soon submitted a résumé, and ended up being hired for a career-changing position. In fact, that crazy event eventually led to what he now refers to as his lifelong dream job.

The reverse is also true: Employees can lose jobs for a myriad of reasons. What's your worst-case scenario? Suppose you were fired from your last major job—and it's the only significant job on your Masterlist. Suppose you deserved the dismissal—you called in too many times with a lame excuse for not showing up. Or maybe you mouthed off to a bratty kid who dropped an ice cream cone on your foot and then climbed onto the retail display toilet and relieved himself in the showroom where you worked. On the other hand, perhaps you had a good idea for changing the way some things were done in a factory and nevertheless got terminated because your brilliant suggestions made your boss look bad.

You get my point: There are all kinds of reasons not only for why people get hired but also for why they get laid off or fired or simply fail to succeed in a given career. So unless you have a history of getting terminated on the basis of your own irresponsibility, one or two "problems" on your employment record shouldn't be overly concerning. Just move on, learning from the past. Don't hide the experiences, but don't dwell on them, either. Living in the past is no way to excel in a future career.

If you need an infusion of self-confidence, consider this: The best way to get advice on the fine points of your résumé is to talk with a couple of people who are already in your chosen field. Just ask around, especially among family and friends, to find such individuals. Ordinarily they'll be glad to help—as long as you don't call them at home in the early hours of a Saturday morning. They were once in your shoes, and chances are you'll one day be in theirs, ready to help a sheepish college student who shows up at your door.

Thanks, by the way, for showing up at my "door." I hope I've helped you pursue your dreams enthusiastically and wisely. If so, drop me a note. I need the encouragement, too. After all, others' encouragement led me to write this book.

Appendices

LIFE EXPERIENCE:	
WHAT, WHEN, AND WHY	Describe here *what* you did, *when* you did it, and *why* you did it.
SKILLS	Describe here what you learned to *do*.
KNOWLEDGE	Describe here what you learned *about*.
TRAITS	Describe here what you learned about *yourself*.

LIFE EXPERIENCE:	
WHAT, WHEN, AND WHY	
SKILLS	
KNOWLEDGE	
TRAITS	

Appendix A

LIST OF POSITIVE TRAITS AS ADJECTIVES

Able **
Accepting **
Accommodating
Accomplished **
Accurate
Active
Adaptable
Adept
Adventurous
Agreeable **
Alert
Ambitious
Analytical
Approachable **
Apt
Articulate
Artistic
Assertive
Attentive
Bold
Bright *
Business-like
Calm **
Candid **
Capable
Careful
Caring **
Cheerful **
Clear-thinking
Committed
Compassionate **
Competent
Competitive
Composed
Confident
Congenial
Conscientious **

Considerate **
Consistent **
Constructive
Convincing *
Cooperative **
Courageous *
Courteous **
Creative
Curious **
Decisive
Dedicated
Dependable **
Detail-oriented
Determined
Devoted **
Dignified *
Diligent
Diplomatic
Direct
Discerning
Disciplined
Discrete
Distinguished *
Dutiful
Dynamic
Eager **
Earnest
Easygoing **
Educated *
Effective
Efficient
Eloquent
Encouraging*
Energetic
Enterprising
Enthusiastic
Ethical

Exacting
Experienced **
Expert *
Expressive
Extroverted
Fair-minded
Faithful **
Flexible
Focused
Forceful
Forthright
Frank **
Friendly
Frugal
Generous
Gentle **
Genuine *
Giving
Good **
Good-natured
Graceful **
Gracious
Gregarious
Happy **
Hardworking
Healthy **
Helpful **
Honest
Hopeful **
Hospitable
Humble *
Humorous **
Informed
Imaginative
Incisive *
Independent
Industrious

* Denotes words that may be perceived as boastful depending upon your skills and résumé content.

162

List of Positive Traits as Adjectives

Innovative
Insightful
Inspiring *
Intellectual *
Intelligent *
Intuitive
Inventive
Investigative
Kind **
Knowledgeable
Learned *
Level-headed
Lively **
Logical
Loving **
Loyal **
Mature
Methodical
Meticulous
Modest *
Motivated
Obedient **
Objective
Observant
Optimistic
Orderly
Organized
Outgoing
Patient
Peace-loving**
Perceptive
Persevering
Persistent
Personable
Persuasive
Pleasant **
Poised

Polite
Popular *
Positive
Practical
Precise
Proactive
Productive
Professional
Proficient
Profit-minded
Profit-oriented
Progressive
Prolific
Prompt
Prudent
Punctual
Purposeful
Qualified
Quick **
Quick-thinking
Rational **
Realistic
Reflective **
Reliable **
Resilient
Resolute
Resourceful
Respectful
Responsible
Self-assured
Self-aware
Self-confident
Self-controlled
Self-motivated
Self-reliant
Self-sufficient
Sensitive **

Sincere **
Serious
Sharp *
Skillful
Smart *
Sociable **
Social **
Steady **
Successful **
Success-oriented
Supportive **
Sympathetic **
Systematic
Tactful
Talented *
Team-oriented
Tenacious
Thorough
Thoughtful
Trusting **
Trustworthy **
Undaunted *
Understanding **
Versatile
Vigorous
Warm **
Well-educated *
Well-organized
Well-trained
Well-versed
Willing **
Wise *

** Denotes words that tend to be too general/generic or too informal or that are overused on résumés.

SKILLS	KNOWLEDGE	TRAITS

KEYWORDS FOR THE JOB OR POSITION YOU SEEK:

SUMMARY STATEMENT:

Summary Statement Worksheet

SKILLS	KNOWLEDGE	TRAITS
planning	event planning A-Z	resourceful
Software	MS Office Suite	accurate
ordering	Supply inventory and requisition	timely
budgeting	Cost-cutting options	thrifty
marketing	Publicity and promos	Creative

KEYWORDS FOR THE JOB OR POSITION YOU SEEK:

Administrative assistant for a nonprofit entity

SUMMARY STATEMENT:

A resourceful administrative professional seeks to serve a local nonprofit to ensure cost-effective operations and increased fund-raising opportunities.

Composed of your skills, knowledge, and traits, plus keywords reflecting how your prospective employer will benefit.

Summary Statement Worksheet

SKILLS	KNOWLEDGE	TRAITS
software	PowerPoint, Avid, MS Word	skilled
technology	editing, lighting, video production	competent
leadership	coordinate team to complete tasks to meet deadlines	dependable, organized
marketing	make posters, ads	creative

KEYWORDS FOR THE JOB OR POSITION YOU SEEK:

Entry-level marketing and promotions representative

SUMMARY STATEMENT:

New-media production graduate with cutting-edge software skills seeks to serve an advertising agency in a team-oriented environment where excellence is valued.

LIST OF ACTION VERBS

Accomplishing Verbs

Accepted **
Achieved *
Acquainted *
Acquired *
Addressed
Answered **
Applied
Apprised
Assembled
Assured
Attained **
Attended **
Audited
Awarded
Balanced
Brainstormed
Captured
Certified
Closed
Communicated *
Compiled
Completed
Concentrated
Converted
Critiqued
Defined
Delivered
Demonstrated *
Detected
Determined
Discovered **
Dissuaded

Distributed
Earned
Enabled
Ensured
Executed
Exhibited **
Experienced **
Facilitated
Finished **
Focused
Fostered
Founded
Functioned **
Gained
Gave **
Handled **
Honored
Influenced
Inspected
Installed
Interpreted
Justified
Learned *
Located **
Logged
Maintained
Marketed
Mastered
Merchandised
Monitored
Motivated **
Observed
Obtained **
Opened

Operated
Ordered
Packaged
Performed **
Pinpointed
Played
Prepared
Presented
Processed **
Projected
Proposed
Provided **
Purchased
Raised
Reached
Realized **
Received
Recommended
Recorded
Referred
Repaired
Replied
Represented
Resolved
Responded
Routed
Saved
Scheduled
Screened
Secured
Selected **
Sent
Served
Sold

* Denotes words often over-used on résumés.
** Denotes words that are informal, weak, or generic.

List of Action Verbs

Translated
Transported
Traveled *
Treated
Validated
Visited
Worked *

Assisting Verbs
Advised **
Aided
Arbitrated
Assisted **
Cared **
Collaborated
Consulted
Contributed
Coordinated *
Counseled
Encouraged **
Greeted
Guided **
Helped
Hosted
Interacted *
Interfaced **
Liaised
Mediated
Moderated
Offered
Participated *
Partnered
Protected
Served *

Supported *
Upheld
Volunteered **
Welcomed **

Creating Verbs
Articulated
Assembled
Authored
Built **
Charted
Composed *
Conceived
Constructed
Created *
Designed
Developed *
Devised
Duplicated
Fabricated
Fashioned
Formed
Formulated **
Founded
Generated
Initiated
Innovated
Inspired
Introduced **
Invented
Launched
Originated
Pioneered
Planned *

Produced
Shaped
Started *

Improving Verbs
Adapted **
Eliminated
Formalized
Improved *
Modernized
Modified
Reconciled
Reconstructed
Rectified
Reduced *
Remodeled
Reshaped
Resolved
Restored
Revamped
Revised **
Revitalized
Revolutionized
Solved **
Stimulated
Streamlined
Supplemented
Tailored
Updated
Upgraded

Increasing Verbs
Amplified
Augmented

* Denotes words often over-used on résumés.

** Denotes words that are informal, weak, or generic.

Broadened
Enlarged
Expanded *
Expedited
Increased
Strengthened

Managing Verbs
Acted
Administered
Allocated
Appropriated
Approved **
Assigned
Authorized
Awarded
Budgeted
Chaired
Conducted *
Controlled
Counseled
Delegated
Directed
Dispensed **
Distributed **
Empowered
Enacted
Enforced
Ensured
Established
Executed
Facilitated
Forecasted
Governed

Guided
Headed
Hired
Identified **
Implemented
Installed
Instituted
Interviewed
Judged
Led
Managed *
Marketed
Nominated
Planned *
Prescribed
Presided
Promoted
Recruited
Sponsored
Supervised *

Organizing Verbs
Archived
Arranged **
Assembled
Catalogued
Centralized
Classified
Compiled
Consolidated
Coordinated *
Filed *
Grouped **
Incorporated

Integrated
Organized **
Prioritized
Reorganized
Restructured
Summarized
Systematized

Researching Verbs
Analyzed
Assessed *
Calculated
Collected
Compared **
Compiled
Computed
Conducted
Contrasted
Diagnosed
Evaluated
Examined
Experimented
Explored **
Extracted
Gathered
Identified *
Isolated
Interviewed
Investigated
Measured **
Observed
Researched
Reviewed *
Sampled

Screened
Studied
Surveyed
Unearthed

Speaking Verbs
Articulated
Communicated *
Dissuaded
Explained
Informed **
Lectured
Negotiated
Persuaded
Teaching Verbs
Clarified
Coached
Educated
Familiarized *
Instructed *
Mentored
Taught *
Trained
Tutored

Writing Verbs
Authored
Briefed
Composed
Corresponded **
Documented *
Drafted
Edited

Proofread
Publicized
Published
Recorded
Reported
Transcribed
Wrote *

* Denotes words often over-used on résumés.

** Denotes words that are informal, weak, or generic.

Wordy Phrases	Concise Language
Participated in study abroad program in Honduras, where I lived with a native family, took courses in Latin American literature and history as well as Honduran culture, and traveled to El Salvador, Guatemala, and Nicaragua, fall 20XX.	Lived with native family while studying and traveling in Latin America during fall 20XX.
Volunteered once a week at a children's home for 30 orphans and children whose parents could no longer take care of them. While I was there, I held infants, played with toddlers, and formed friendships with many adolescent girls in need of love and positive attention.	Provided weekly role modeling, friendship, and interaction at 30-resident children's home.
Completed tasks within a team environment, often requiring working through the night to meet deadlines.	Worked overtime with team to meet tight deadlines.
Placed multi-formatted advertisements in a variety of media throughout the city of Chicago.	Placed multi-formatted ads throughout Chicago media.
Multitasked while under pressure in the restaurant's high-paced, busy atmosphere, which called for thinking on my feet and handling stress.	Multitasked in a fast-paced, high-pressure restaurant.

Appendix E

Wordy Phrases	Concise Language
Welcomed and seated assorted customers and presented a great first impression for the clientele for the restaurant.	Warmly welcomed and seated guests.
Maintained constant and open communication with other hosts in order to give accurate "quote" times during a wait as well as to avoid overloading servers.	Collaborated with cohosts to ensure accurate seating-time estimates and efficient distribution of customers among servers.
Functioned as a leader over the hosts when necessary, while being able to take orders at other times for optimal operation as a team.	Alternated between hosting and serving to ensure customer satisfaction.
Acquired life lessons about working with a team and getting the job done with precision and excellence.	Acquired valuable team experience to meet objectives.
Selected best shots after days of filming for other editors to cut into finished product.	Recommended best camera shots for editors.
Oversaw entire staff (writers, photographers, and copy editors) during biweekly production nights of weekly school paper.	Supervised entire school paper staff during biweekly production.

Wordy Phrases	Concise Language
Served on college Student Life Committee at ABC College, helping to determine what new changes might be implemented in residence halls for the good of the student body.	Served on Student Life Committee that planned and implemented residence hall improvements.
Served as camera operator covering campus-wide events, such as the Shakespearean Plays Festival. First play can be found at http://www.webaddress.can.	Video recorded campus-wide events, such as Shakespearean Plays Festival (www.webaddress.can).
Worked efficiently while working under many various departments.	Served 6 departments efficiently and effectively.
Developed appreciation for the unique stories of individuals at diverse moments in life.	Gained appreciation for others' unique life experiences.
Raised over 400 dollars for the World Relief Organization of my church for aid in Myanmar with minimum cost by using persuasive tactics to gather donations from students.	Persuaded students to donate $400 to world relief organization.
Aiding 2 professors with various projects, including works-cited list for soon-to-be-published text and college's rhetoric-across-the-curriculum program.	Assisting 2 professors with bibliographic and teaching projects.

Appendix E

Wordy Phrases	Concise Language
Provided spiritual and emotional support for 160 women while living with them in residence hall.	Provided spiritual and emotional support for 160 dorm women.
Conducted internal research project to aid nonprofit organization in development of more strategic approach to relationships with supporting organizations.	Researched nonprofit's relationships with supporting organizations for strategic plan.
Traveled on short-term mission trips to Puerto Rico; Peru; Jamaica; Mexico; and Philadelphia, PA (20XX–20XX), developing a fuller understanding of the world, different cultures, and poverty.	Gained a fuller understanding of cultural diversity and poverty while traveling on 5 international, short-term mission trips in 5 years.
Volunteered at a school in downtown Denver; helped kids after school with homework and played games.	Voluntarily assisted with tutoring and recreational activities at urban school.
Shot and edited wedding video for a friend and created a DVD for her and her family (December 20XX).	Produced and edited wedding video and created DVD memoir.
Assisted in coordinating and setting up of precollege workshops and seminars for urban churches.	Helped set up and coordinate precollege programs for urban congregations.

Wordy Phrases	Concise Language
Experience with demographic research, niche marketing, out-of-the-box marketing concepts, strong leadership, and team-building skills.	Gained experience with market research, leadership, and team-building skills.
Went to professional sporting events with the sports director, where I was allowed to interview professional athletes.	Interviewed professional athletes at events supervised by sports director.
Open and closed, while dealing with hundreds of dollars daily. Fast-paced environment while working with customers and taking on the responsibility of helping run a family business.	Handled money for and helped manage a fast-paced family business.
Helped find bands that were hired for live entertainment and made performances run smoothly.	Selected live bands and ensured smooth performances.
Cocreated and executed the advertising campaign for 20XX Fall Dance Club show, the biggest sell-out of Dance Club history.	Cocreated and executed advertising campaign for record-breaking dance performance.
Analyzed information gathered through interviews to formulate report outlining research findings and suggestions for future action.	Analyzed and reported research findings and suggested future action.

Appendix E

Wordy Phrases	Concise Language
Gained greater understanding of nonprofit work through mentoring meetings, involvement in office life, and intentional relationships with staff.	Learned nonprofit teamwork.
Ensured that rooms were set up properly and equipped for each workshop or seminar.	Ensured proper setup and equipping for events.
Prepared an illustrated spreadsheet with colored graphics so that salespeople would see the premium potential available by county and insurable product line across the entire country.	Created color-coded spreadsheet of company's national premium potential by county and product line.

Words

"To" and "**too**" (going someplace vs. in addition to, also, or excessive)

- I went **to** Cool College.
- I understand your marketing director graduated from there, **too**.

"**Its**" and "**it's**" (possessive vs. contraction of "it is"). Note that this is the exception to the rule that *'s* forms are possessives).

- My résumé should distinguish itself by **its** content.
- **It's** well known that your corporation is at the leading edge of technology.

"**There**," "**their**," and "**they're**" (place vs. possessive vs. contraction of "they are")

- **There** are numerous reasons I would like to serve your organization.
- Information for references includes **their** e-mail addresses for your convenience.
- **They're** ready to speak with you about what skills I would bring to your company.

"**Your**" and "**you're**" (possessive vs. contraction of "you are")

- **Your** organization's philanthropic focus is highly regarded.
- **You're** at the top of every list of companies that spend very little to raise considerable funds.

"**A lot**" and "**alot**" (the latter is generally not accepted as a word)

- I have **a lot** of experience with research and development within your specialty.
- "**Alot**" is not a word and shouldn't appear in your cover letter or on your résumé.

"**Insure**" and "**ensure**" (promising money as "insurance" vs. making a guarantee of performance)

- My former company **insure**d property against loss by natural disaster.
- My job was to **ensure** that customers got the best service possible when they filed a claim.

Capitalization

When indicating an academic major, observe traditional rules for capitalization. Languages and specific locations are capitalized; all others are not. Official department names are capitalized, but other references to specific departments are not.

- Earned English major and economics minor
- Completed major in the Department of English (or "English department" when not referring to department by name)
- Studied in the Department of Near Eastern Languages

Also distinguish between headline and sentence capitalization. In *headline capitalization*, every word is capitalized, except for prepositions, articles (*a, an*, or *the*), and adverbs (*to* and *as*).

- B.A., Eighteenth-Century English History, Almsden College
- Assistant to Secretary, Department of Geology, Fall 20XX–Spring 20XX

In *sentence capitalization*, capitalize only the first word, all proper nouns, the pronoun "I," and certain abbreviations and acronyms:

- Graduated with B.A. in eighteenth-century English history from Almsden College.
- Worked as assistant to secretary for the geology department (or Department of Geology), fall 20XX–spring 20XX.

Periods

In *bulleted* text, normally use periods only after a complete sentence (with a subject and verb).

- I am proficient in Hemhaw Pro 20XX for Windows.
- Proficient in Hemhaw Pro 20XX for Windows
- Entered new-customer records; ensured clean, professional-looking lounge area; maintained safe walking surfaces in winter.

Consistency

When describing your current and past experiences, be grammatically consistent.

- Responsible for stocking shelves, rotating perishable items, and checking prices (*current* experiences)
- Contributed to school paper; fielded technical support requests; tutored ESL students (*past* experiences)

Numbers

In order to keep your résumé concise and to save space, use digits rather than spelled-out numbers whenever possible.

- Counseled 23 children in a 2-week summer camp for 11- and 12-year-olds

But *never* choose conciseness over readability. When necessary, spell out numbers for clarity.

- Attended two 4-day seminars (*or* Attended 2 four-day seminars)

Ampersands

Even though space on a résumé can be tight, write out the word *and*, reserving the **ampersand** (&) for existing proper nouns.

- Marketing Intern, Simon **&** Schuster, Inc.
- Graduated from Texas A&M University

Date

Name
Company
Address
City, ST Zip

Dear Ms. Johnson:

I am writing to apply for the advertised opening in customer service at Comfy Cozy Bed and Breakfast. I saw the advertisement in *The Daily Press* and on monster.com while searching for a position in the bed and breakfast industry.

My experience matches the skills and traits listed in your advertisement and evident on your website.

First, I possess the necessary cross-cultural skills and experience you listed for this position. I am conversationally adept in Spanish, Dutch, and American Sign Language. I can also read some German, French, and Italian.

Second, I have managed complex projects and relationships in a residential organization. While a resident assistant at Mejan College, I was responsible for 40 young women's personal, social, and educational growth through dormitory activities and hospitality. For nine months I worked with floor leaders and residents to make our dormitory community one of the most resident-friendly and supportive social environments on campus. I learned about the many different, sometimes conflicting, needs of individuals, including their needs for rest, relaxation, quiet, information, and privacy.

Third, I know the activities that visitors of all ages are likely to enjoy in the wider community. I have served as a camp counselor and activities teacher, a tour guide at a chocolate factory, and the sole proprietor of my own summer garden care company. I know the kinds of activities and settings that make for enjoyable leisure time. In addition, I have assisted people with special physical needs.

I look forward to discussing with you the various ways in which I could help accomplish your goals for Comfy Cozy Bed and Breakfast. My enclosed résumé includes additional information about my related experience.

Sincerely,

Lydia Hulst
Address
Phone
E-mail

LYDIA HULST

CURRENT (until 12/20XX):
Mejan College, Vella Hall
2222 Buxton NE
Jongsma, GA 30999
(222) 333-4444
student@college.edu

PERMANENT:
8888 Waters Way
Jeffers, GA 30888
(777) 888-9999
(444) 555-1111 (cell)
permanent@home.com

SUMMARY

A hospitable, motivated, and creative individual with cross-cultural experience seeks to assist the staff of Comfy Cozy Bed and Breakfast with exemplary guest service, stellar cuisine, and superb garden appearance.

EDUCATION

Bachelor of Arts in Communication (May 20XX)

Mejan College, Jongsma, GA

- Honors student
- January 20XX course: Be Fit for Life—Bike Australia
- Studied Spanish, American Sign Language, and Dutch
- Six scholarships

EXPERIENCE

Coast-to-Coast Bike Tour (Summer 20XX)

- Bicycled 4,000 miles from Seattle to Jersey City to raise awareness and funds
- Collected over $10,000 for the poor
- Led small-group meetings for interpersonal support

Resident Assistant (Fall 20XX–Spring 20XX)

Mejan College, Jongsma, GA

- Contributed to personal growth and education of 40 college women
- Provided support and information for all dormitory residents
- Organized social, educational, and spiritually focused activities
- Participated in weekly dormitory leadership meetings
- Directed biweekly floor board meetings
- Mentored student leaders
- Interviewed candidates for resident assistant positions 20XX–20XX

Office Assistant, Language Department (Spring 20XX–present)

Mejan College, Jongsma, GA

- Performed organizational and data input tasks for faculty

182

Agriculture Building Greenhouse Caretaker (Fall 20XX)
Mejan College, Jongsma, GA
- Watered, weeded, and maintained the college conservatory

Counselor (Summers 20XX and 20XX)
Camp Jones, Welker, GA
- Counseled girls between the ages of 8 and 16 for 9 weeks
- Taught water ballet, boating, fishing, archery, and wilderness survival
- Served as a Red Cross certified lifeguard for daily free swims
- Assisted campers with special physical needs

Tour Guide (Summers 20XX and 20XX)
Candy Cookers Center, Veenstra, GA
- Facilitated age-appropriate tours of chocolate factory
- Provided quality customer service as knowledgeable sales assistant
- Ensured inviting store appearance and availability of products

Flower Care Entrepreneur (Summers 20XX and 20XX)
Self-Employed, Veenstra, GA
- Developed a client base through effective advertising and customer referrals
- Provided weekly garden care for summer residents
- Managed all scheduling and accounting

ACTIVITIES

Mejan College
- Completed 3-week service-learning trip to post-Katrina Louisiana (winter 20XX)
- Led "Celebrate the Block Fest 20XX" team
- Assisted with "So Cool Dorm Leadership—Partners in Community" program

Date

Name
Company
Address
City, ST Zip

Dear Mr. Chimienti:

I am writing to apply for the community marketing position with the Streaks professional soccer team. I saw the advertisement in the local press and in *Professional Soccer* magazine. The job description posted on your team's website lists many qualifications that I possess. Moreover, I have multimedia skills that will help a team like yours with essential online promotion.

I learned about sports marketing while traveling across Michigan as a crew member on the Konyndyk Demo Tour. While distributing Konyndyk products for consumer trial and collaborating with the company's marketing team to promote Konyndyk sports equipment, I learned about the importance of forming positive relationships among sports teams, equipment manufacturers, local communities, fans, and the media. As a member of the Konyndyk team, I worked long nights and every weekend to ensure campaign success.

Furthermore, I am a goal-oriented, self-motivated person who loves to excel, especially in sports-related work. I have taught soccer basics and promoted the sport as a team-building, health-promoting activity for children and parents.

My skills also include writing, producing, and editing for numerous media. I have a solid grasp of the Microsoft Office Suite.

Also, I know how to collaborate on successful projects. I facilitated team building as a soccer and track coach for the Roseboro Public Schools. I worked with a construction crew in high-pressure situations to complete jobs on time, regardless of weather conditions and employee illnesses.

I would love to interview with you to find out more about this and any other entry-level positions with the Streaks. My attached résumé further highlights my experience, education, and skills.

Sincerely,

David K. Wales

Address
Phone
E-mail

David K. Wales

9999 Griffin Court SE, Engels, GA 31111
(111) 222-5555
permanent@home.com

SUMMARY

A goal-oriented, self-motivated problem solver with multimedia skills seeks to join an innovative sports marketing team.

EXPERIENCE

Worthy Construction Corp., Heeringa, MI
Steel Framer, Summer 20XX–Fall 20XX
- Gained a strong work ethic at a demanding job
- Collaborated with a team in high-pressure situations to complete all tasks on schedule

Konyndyk Demo Tour, Heeringa, MI
Crew Member, Winter 20XX–Spring 20XX
- Distributed Konyndyk products for consumer trial
- Worked with marketing team to promote Konyndyk equipment

Roseboro Public Schools, Holquist, GA
Soccer and Track Coach, Spring and Fall 20XX
- Taught basic soccer and running exercises
- Promoted healthy lifestyles to students and parents
- Facilitated sports team-building

EDUCATION

Pinsky College, Hubbard, IA
B.A., Business Communication, Spring 20XX
- Completed across-the-curriculum writing program
- Performed industry analysis to confirm an organization's decision to expand
- 20XX Leiter Leadership Conference participant
- 20XX Bruner Research Essay winner

TECHNOLOGY

- Advanced skills with Microsoft Word, Excel, PowerPoint, and Publisher

Date

Name
Company
Address
City, ST Zip

Dear Ms. Orkar:

I am writing to apply for the position of audio editor at XYZ Audio Services. My former college roommate and now area videographer, Jim Sheetz, told me about your company and encouraged me to apply. After reviewing your website and listening to recordings of your clients' music, I concluded that XYZ's philosophy, clients, and technology would be an excellent fit with my own experience and skills.

Like XYZ Audio Services, I specialize primarily in musical recording. I have considerable experience in college and conference recording of live events, including meetings, multimedia lectures, band performances, and prerecorded music. I have recorded musical material in a wide range of venues, focusing on both live audio and recorded soundtracks. In addition, I appreciate nearly all musical styles and attend many concerts, where I arrive early to investigate the ways in which audio engineers mike and mix for venues, performers, and recording equipment.

I also share XYZ's emphasis on Pro Tools–related technology. While I have learned other software and related hardware, I invested my college and post-college activities in learning Pro Tools for audio and soundtrack recordings. I know the menus for using Pro Tools in both Windows and Mac environments. I am also skilled in Pro Tools' companion video software, Avid Composer.

I would like to contribute to XYZ's industry-leading work in integrating the Internet with audio editing. I am excited about the trend toward multisite collaboration through secure Web servers. Given the growing cost of hosting musicians and producers in one location for long periods of time, online collaboration offers financial advantages.

My enclosed résumé and CD sampler reflect my skills, knowledge, and traits. I believe that I would be a good fit for XYZ. I hope to hear from you soon about a possible interview.

Sincerely,

James Kool Smith

Address
Phone
E-mail

James Kool Smith

♦ 2711 Overstreet Blvd., Koopmans, AZ 86666 ♦
♦ (111) 222-4444 ♦ www.jameskoolmedia.usa ♦ contact@jameskool.usa ♦

SUMMARY

A self-motivated, hard-working, experienced audio engineer who is passionate about music seeks to serve the recording industry.

EXPERIENCE

Kool Media Productions USA, Glenny, AZ   Fall 20XX–Present
Owner/Operator
- Designing audio projects
- Recording original material
- Shooting and editing promotional video projects
- Developing www.jameskoolmedia.usa

M. Smith Thespian Theatre, Mountaintop, AZ
Sound Technician   Fall 20XX–Present
- Setting up and tearing down audio recording equipment
- Running mixer for weekly events
- Duplicating DVDs of theatrical productions

Padjen College, Mountaintop, AZ
Technical Services Sound Technician   Fall 20XX–Present
- Setting up audio equipment prior to event
- Running sound check for acts and operating mixer for events
- Providing technical support for lectures and musicians
- Recording live shows
- Operating video switcher and other multimedia equipment

Vos Conference Center, Lindvall, AZ
Conference Assistant   Summer 20XX and 20XX
- Ran sound and lighting for various conferences
- Set up conference rooms
- Provided technical support to conference leaders
- Ensured smooth-running conferences

Badzinski Conference Center, Kristy, AZ
Independent Audio Contractor   Fall 20XX–Summer 20XX
- Operated front-of-house mixer for annual meeting of 300+ college faculty

James Kool Smith (111) 222-4444
www.jameskoolmedia.usa

TECHNOLOGY

- Proficient in Windows and Mac OS
- Experienced in Office for Windows and Mac
- Competent in Pro Tools and Audition recording/editing software
- Skilled in Avid Media Composer
- Qualified on digital and analog boards
- Knowledgeable in Web design, including Windows FrontPage 20XX; Adobe Dreamweaver; basic HTML, JavaScript, and cascading style sheets

EDUCATION

Padjen College, Mountaintop, AZ
B.A., Music major
- Designed a mock radio show
- Recorded original 6-track music
- Created commercials, facilitated banter, and conducted a recorded interview
- Developed audio signatures for Kool Media Productions USA
- Created sample ring tones and click tones
- Completed courses at York St. John University, York, England (spring 20XX)

ACTIVITIES

- Played drums with church band
- Learned guitar
- Gained multicultural experience traveling to Nice, France, and Dublin, Ireland
- Participated in a short-term service project in Montego Bay, Jamaica (20XX)

CERTIFICATIONS AND ASSOCIATIONS

- Student Member of the Audio Engineers Society
- CPR/AED certified
- "G" class license

Date

Name
Company
Address
City, ST Zip

Dear Mr. VanderMeer:

I am writing to apply for the public relations assistant account manager position distributed through the alumni network of my college. I have reviewed the job description posted on your firm's website and conducted a Google news search for all of the articles mentioning your company during the past five years. My combination of skills, knowledge, and traits fits both your current job openings and your client profile.

During and after college I developed my skills as an organized, positive team builder. As my résumé shows, I have helped for-profit and nonprofit teams with short-term and long-term projects. I have worked with local media, neighborhood associations, a chamber of commerce, and numerous retail businesses. I have managed schedules, planned meetings, organized special events, and coordinated workshops.

Moreover, I am self-motivated. I love working hard and find great satisfaction in completing tasks. While working as an organizer for the City Neighborhood Association, I took on projects that were well beyond what was required for the position. In Wilson, Texas, I created a new neighborhood organization that is now serving local citizens. While working there, I also designed a plan for future summer interns to continue the work I had begun.

I know the importance and dynamics of public relations in the community. I recognize the importance of businesses, government, and citizens' groups understanding each other.

Thank you for considering my application and a possible interview. I would be delighted to provide additional information beyond my attached résumé.

Sincerely,

Sara Haagen

Address
Phone
E-mail

Sara Haagen

Present
Mast College
9999 Veenstra Ave.
Wieland, TX 77999
(333) 777-6000

Permanent
4444 Webster Road
Westra, IN 46666
(777) 666-5555
permanent@e-mail.com

SUMMARY

A self-motivated, organized, positive leader with team-building experience
seeks to serve a public relations firm.

EXPERIENCE

Alliance Business Network, Wilson, TX

Public Relations Manager / Student Intern (September 20XX–Present)

Publicized business district's Annual Autumn Stroll. Collaborated with chamber of commerce to promote zoning enforcement.

Citywide Neighborhood Association, Wilson, TX

Student Organizer / PR Campaign Manager for Ottawa District (May 20XX–May 20XX)

Encouraged home ownership in commercial and residential districts. Partnered with colleges to promote modern living in the neighborhood through special chamber of commerce events. Created the Worthy Heights Organization and coordinated, promoted, and emceed their Chippewa Block Party.

Korff Salon and Spa, Wilson, TX

Guest Services Coordinator (May 20XX–March 20XX)

Managed schedules, made reservations, entered inventory data, and assisted guests. Acquired team-building skills while providing sales support.

Haute Couture, Inc., New York, NY

Corporate Intern (Summer 20XX)

Assisted merchandising team with advertising, product placement, packaging, pricing, and shipping.

Student Volunteer Service, Rodney College, Last Plains, TX

Pre-college Programs Assistant (Winter 20XX)

Helped set up and coordinate workshops and seminars for high-school seniors.

Sara Haagen

ACTIVITIES

Career Workshop for Women with a Mission

Conducted mini career workshop for 10th- through 12th-grade female students.

ABC Event Planning, Marketing, and Design Partnership

Project Coordinator, Creative Director

Organized and advertised Poetic Progress fundraiser for public school district.

Annual Fundraisers for Local Community Schools

Sponsored by Bamford Bank. Coordinated and directed three successful fashion shows (20XX–20XX). Raised over $1500 for public school art program and college art scholarship. Created PowerPoint presentations, prepared budget reports, and finalized sponsor invoices.

ADDITIONAL EXPERIENCE

Proficient with Microsoft Word, Excel, PowerPoint, and Internet Explorer. Understand demographic research, niche marketing, out-of-the-box marketing concepts, leadership, and team building.

Date

Name
Company
Address
City, ST Zip

Dear Ms. Sharp:

I am writing to apply for the internship in speech-language pathology at your hospital. Having completed my undergraduate degree in speech-language pathology, I hope to learn more about the field through an internship at your respected hospital. My strong cross-cultural interests, bilingual skills, and focus on serving children fit your job description posted on the American Speech-Language-Hearing Association's website.

While working on my B.A. in speech-language pathology and audiology at Schut College, I combined professional studies with cross-cultural engagement. I tutored a Korean woman in English, studied the effects of bilingual education on children with Specific Language Impairment, and lived and volunteered in Latin America.

I became fluent in Spanish as my second language in order to better serve future clients from Latin America. I lived in Latin America so that I could experience another culture firsthand. Along the way, I gained a special appreciation for the difficulties of bilingual children with speech difficulties.

As my résumé indicates, I completed over twenty hours of observation in speech pathology and audiology evaluation and treatment, achieved the dean's list nearly every semester, developed my verbal and written reporting skills, and conducted some of my own client assessments under careful supervision. While I am qualified to apply for a master's degree in the field, I would prefer to intern before proceeding to graduate school.

I am passionate about serving children and view this internship as an opportunity to serve your young clients, as well as to prepare for graduate school.

Thank you for considering my application. Please let me know if you would like any additional information beyond what is already covered in the attached résumé.

Sincerely,

Colleen Poel

Address
Phone
E-mail

COLLEEN POEL

9999 Mark St. SE
Peters, MA 01111

(XXX) 444-6666
permanent@home.com

SUMMARY: A compassionate, proactive, bilingual speech-language pathology graduate desires a hospital internship to learn more about serving children with language and learning disabilities and oral motor deficits.

EDUCATION: **Schut College**, Rowe, MA
- Earned a B.A. in Speech-Language Pathology and Audiology with Spanish minor in December 20XX
- Lived with native family while studying and traveling in Latin America during fall 20XX
- Tutored Korean woman in English weekly (fall 2005)
- Observed 20 hours of speech pathology and audiology evaluation and treatment
- Achieved dean's list for 7 semesters
- Gained proficiency in SALT software for speech analysis
- Studied effects of bilingual education on children with Specific Language Impairment

EXPERIENCE: **Schut College**, Rowe, MA
Student Clinician, Fall 20XX
- Designed evaluation activities for a stroke client and administered therapy
- Developed verbal and written reporting skills
- Increased proficiency in data collection and analysis

Test Assistant, Spring 20XX
- Administered, scored, and analyzed Clinical Evaluation of Language Fundamentals (Fourth Edition), Peabody Picture Vocabulary Test, Comprehensive Test of Phonological Processes, and Gray Oral Readings Test
- Recorded, transcribed, and analyzed language samples of two young boys

Beacon Estates, Woods, MA
Part-time Relief Receptionist, Fall 20XX–Present
- Answer phones, welcome visitors, sort and deliver mail

Instituto Hondureño, *Honduras*
Volunteer, Fall 20XX
- Provided positive role modeling, friendship, and interaction for residents of children's home

Date

Name
Company
Address
City, ST Zip

Dear Ms. Valkenburg:

I recently met Byron Vos at a local meeting of the Advertising Club of America, and he informed me that you might be looking for an entry-level employee at the JJ Agency.

I know from my own research that your agency serves international clients, and I believe that my skills and experience could serve your agency in the increasingly global marketplace.

As my attached résumé indicates, in the last few years I have examined global business practices in seven different European countries. I also lived for three months in the Czech Republic, where I studied international marketing, management, and economics.

I founded an economics club at Toering College, using my strong interpersonal skills to gain the college administration's support. I promoted the club on campus and personally scheduled the first six campus speakers.

My experience also includes work with an automobile dealership that sells new and pre-owned imports. Before that, I learned much about retail by becoming a top-selling footwear salesperson.

I believe that my strong interpersonal skills, customer-relations experience, and international background would serve your agency well. Please let me know about a possible interview with your agency.

Sincerely,

Ellen White Stegenga

Address
Phone
E-mail

ELLEN WHITE STEGENGA

99 Forest Grove, Tolbert, IN
Phone: (777) 899-2211 ● E-mail: tfitz@drqbook.com

SUMMARY
A strong interpersonal communicator with multicultural and customer relations experience desires to serve an international advertising agency.

EXPERIENCE

Rose Automotive, Storteboom SC
Intern
February 20XX–May 20XX
Helped salespersons increase customer satisfaction indexes for Jaguar, Land Rover, and BMW automobiles. Mastered the product database programs of each manufacturer.

Rose Automotive, Storteboom SC
Porter
June 20XX–December 20XX
Picked up customers, performed detailing services, and delivered clients' vehicles.

Tanis Outdoors, Klompen, IN
Sales Associate
February 20XX–December 20XX
Sold men's and women's footwear, set up displays, organized inventory, and resolved customer complaints. Consistent top seller in department.

Redeemer Church, Sudlow, IN
Worship Leader
September 20XX–June 20XX
Coordinated worship band, planned rehearsals, and led worship services.

EDUCATION

Toering College, Tol, SC
B.A. Business (May 20XX)

20XX Globalization and Culture Study, Europe
Examined global business practices in 7 different countries. Studied the history and culture of Europe.

20XX International University, Prague, Czech Republic
Studied international marketing, management, and economics in a multicultural setting with a focus on group work. Lived with roommates from 4 cultures.

Toering College International Business Club, Tol, SC
Founder and Chair
Founded and created an organization for Toering students to learn more about international business. Promoted group and scheduled 6 camp speakers.

Date

Name
Company
Address
City, ST Zip

Dear Mr. Creasman:

I am writing to apply for the position of geological assistant at the Seismic Institute. I saw the advertisement for the position in the classified section of *Geographer* magazine. After reviewing your institute's website and reading essays published by some of your staff, I concluded that I could serve the mission and purpose of the Seismic Institute.

As my attached résumé and the enclosed DVD indicate, I have been studying geology for the last four years. During this time I completed three on-site, all-summer geological research projects. I recorded, edited, and produced a DVD on the geology of western Montana; that DVD is now being used to introduce college students to the ongoing fieldwork in that region. I also served as a research assistant to faculty in the college's geology department.

In addition, I have developed strong organizational skills by volunteering at and working for nonprofit organizations. I was a team leader for a religious community, where I also taught fourth-graders from the neighborhood. My work as a geological studies apprentice included planning and leading weekly meetings of current and prospective geology majors. I studied American Sign Language as a means of collaborating with the deaf community.

My cross-cultural experience includes teaching English as a second language to new, primarily Hispanic immigrants at a YMCA in Texas. While serving as an intern at a religious community in California, I worked with an ethnically and generationally diverse community.

I would love to talk with you more about how I might contribute to the success of the Seismic Institute. Thank you for considering my application and a possible interview.

Sincerely,

Jackson K. White

Address
Phone
E-mail

JACKSON K. WHITE

CURRENT (UNTIL 5/20XX):
888 Maple Street
Bosmeyer, CT 06999
Phone: XXX-333-2222
jkwhite@permmail.usa

PERMANENT:
1728 Ironside Ct.
Jake, CT 06888
Phone: XXX-333-1111
Fax: XXX-333-1112

SUMMARY: A self-motivated geologist with strong organizational skills, significant research experience, and extensive exposure to multicultural settings seeks to collaborate with other geologists at a nonprofit research and educational organization.

EDUCATION:
B.S. in Geology, Music Minor (May 20XX)
Carmody College, Cater, CT
- Recorded, edited, and produced DVD on geology of western Montana
- Studied American Sign Language for 3 years
- Completed 3 on-site, all-summer geological research projects

EXPERIENCE:
Geology Department Research Assistant, September 20XX to Present
Carmody College, Cater, CT
- Organizing data entry for current projects and classes
- Assisting in academic research and teaching introductory geology course

Chapel Fellow, February 20XX to Present (part-time)
Carmody College, Cater, CT
- Studying the benefits and challenges of chapel ministry
- Proming unity of campus leadership via participation in campus worship, prayer, and meditation

Ministry Intern, June 20XX to August 20XX
Praise Community Church, Coksville, CA
- Led worship services for ethnically and generationally diverse congregation
- Co-taught 4th-grade class for outreach program serving families
- Planned curriculum for backyard clubs and helped coordinate small teams

Geological Studies Apprentice, August 20XX to May 20XX
Carmody College, Cater, CT
- Planned and led weekly meetings of current and prospective geology majors
- Recruited new majors for special summer geological survey program

ESL Tutor, September 20XX to December 20XX
YMCA, Cornwell, TX
- Taught English language basics to new immigrants
- Answered cultural questions about life in the United States

Appendix G

Date

Name
Company
Address
City, PR Zip

Dear Ms. McLaughlin:

I am writing to submit my résumé for position #1024 in Internet marketing at your highly respected company.

I know from my extensive online research and personal discussions with one of your employees that your organization is on the leading edge of Internet-based marketing. I also know that you were listed in *Net Promo* magazine as one of the top 50 places to work because of your support of achievement-oriented employees.

I am applying, first, because I believe that I am the kind of self-motivated, highly organized employee you seek. During the last three years I have diligently sought to learn the many aspects of Internet marketing by serving as an Internet correspondent, a marketing and promotion assistant, a marketing intern with responsibility for writing online stories, a public relations manager for a college actors' guild, and a contract worker reviewing e-commerce websites. I have worked hard at a wide range of activities, investing evenings and weekends for my own study and practice.

I am also applying for this position because I have the combination of technical and writing skills needed for such cutting-edge work. I am skilled with Adobe software, including Illustrator, Dreamweaver, and Photoshop. I know how to design and maintain user-friendly websites. At the same time, I can write well for online audiences, with short, direct, persuasive prose.

I would greatly appreciate an opportunity to talk with you about the ways in which I could serve your company. My résumé is attached, my personal blog about online marketing is available at www.samdekkermarketing.can, and an expanded online résumé with hyperlinks can be accessed using the password "talsma_marketing" (no quotes) at www.talsmarésumé.can.

Sincerely,

Samantha Dekker Talsma

Address
Phone
E-mail

SAMANTHA DEKKER TALSMA

231 Wood Street, Darling, BC V2T 3Z9
Phone: (555) 444-3333 • Fax: (555) 444-3332 • E-mail: person@home.usa

SUMMARY: A self-motivated, organized, and positive leader with writing experience seeks to serve an Internet marketing organization.

EXPERIENCE: **Internet Correspondent**, *Our Times* Magazine
Detwiler, ON 20XX–present
• Writing articles periodically for the "Media and Culture" section

Marketing and Promotions Assistant, GateWorks International
DeHaan, ON 20XX–present
• Updating website copy, graphics, and database content
• Authoring news stories, developing promotional products, staffing tradeshows

Marketing Department Intern, GateWorks International
DeHaan, ON 20XX (3 months)
• Edited writers' stories for online newsletter
• Conducted secondary and primary research for donor database

Contract Work
• Co-evaluated Southwest Ontario Communications e-commerce site (August 20XX)
• Co-reviewed 8 business websites (August 20XX)

Public Relations Manager, Jenkins College Actors Guild
Toronto, ON 20XX–20XX
• Coordinated, organized, and promoted student-led group of 150 actors

Extern in Media Relations Department, Jeremiah Associates
Mattingly, ON 20XX (one week)
• Assembled media kits, composed press releases, and observed all aspects of media relations

TECHNOLOGY: Skilled with Microsoft Publisher and Word, as well as Adobe Photoshop, Illustrator, and Dreamweaver

EDUCATION: **B.A., Spanish—Jenkins College**
Toronto, ON May 20XX
• Completed advanced Spanish conversation and composition
• Coordinated team of 11 student mentors
• Acquired Web design and development skills

Date

Name
Title
Company
Address
City, ST Zip

Dear Mr. Bruner:

I am writing in response to the middle school teacher position posted on your school's website. I have reviewed the job description carefully and have downloaded and read your school's manuals for teachers and parents. I believe that I would be an excellent candidate for this position.

I am a 20XX Alsdurf College graduate who has been working in area schools for the past three years. As my résumé shows, I have experience in various schools and grade levels, but prefer middle school.

I previously taught sixth grade and enjoyed it very much. I appreciate the challenges and joys of teaching students who are beginning to think deeply about their world. My mentor is an experienced, National Board Certified teacher who has reinforced my desire to be a middle school educator.

I believe I could make a substantial contribution toward helping your school fulfill its mission as a multicultural learning community. Because of my numerous trips abroad and my semester in Spain, I have gained valuable intercultural experience that has served me well in my teaching. As a bilingual educator, I am uniquely qualified to facilitate learning for Hispanic students who may not have learned English as their first language.

I am a compassionate and hard-working educator with significant classroom experience. As a member of your staff, I would dedicate myself to excellence in education on behalf of the students, parents, and staff.

I look forward to your response to my interest in this opportunity. I would love to visit your school.

Best regards,

Benjamin M. Neuman

Address
Phone
E-mail

Benjamin M. Neuman
1111 Mouw Place Court, Metts, FL 33333
permanent@home.com
(333) 555-7777

SUMMARY
A bilingual educator with a love of teaching and extensive multicultural experience seeks to serve a community-oriented school.

EDUCATION
Alsdurf College, Baxter, FL
B.A. Elementary Education, Spanish minor (5/XX); dean's list and Academic Achievement Award every semester.

TEACHING

Kids' Club Teacher (1/XX–present)
Arthurs Spelling School, Ronda, FL
Researching, planning, and implementing enrichment activities for groups of preschool and kindergarten students. Pioneering and growing new program by working with staff, students, and parents.

Sixth Grade Teacher (8/XX–12/XX)
Spencer Charter School Academy, Okenka, FL
Taught English, social studies, spelling, and science to academically diverse class of 19 students.

In-House Substitute and Spanish Teacher (9/XX–6/XX)
Perera Village School, Pope, FL
Tutored, taught, and led 2nd- to 6th-grade groups; planned, prepared, and taught Spanish lessons to 2nd graders.

Substitute Teacher (1/XX–6/XX)
Bennett Township Schools, Prinsen, FL
Performed teaching tasks daily in K–8 classrooms.

Student Teacher (8/XX–12/XX)
Seignious Elementary, Wallace, FL
Taught a challenging 5th-grade class of mainly Hispanic students.

Tutor (6/XX–7/XX)
Ofulue, FL
Wrote and taught half-hour reading lessons to 2nd-grade student.

Student Aide (9/XX–12/XX)
Annalee Ripley School, Spies, FL
Wrote lessons, taught writing and reading, graded papers, tutored students, and provided administrative support for 6th-grade teacher.

VOLUNTEERING

Tutor (11/XX–present)
Turcott Community College ESL Program, Belilsbe, FL
Assisting Hispanic elementary school children with homework, reading, and math.

Children's Worship Assistant (9/XX–present)
Church of the Shepherd, Wainer, FL
Aiding in storytelling, crafts, and songs with culturally diverse groups aged 3–7.

ADDITIONAL

- Gained extensive cross-cultural experience in the Netherlands, Japan, the Czech Republic, Spain, and England.
- Completed Semester in Spain program; lived, traveled and studied in Spain.
- Self-taught in PowerPoint and Word. Experienced with Mac and PC.
- Wrote 3 novels, 6 short stories, and 3 recorded songs.

_____ 1. I completed a Masterlist (appendix A) of my life experiences.

_____ 2. I identified my skills, knowledge, and traits, as evidenced in my Masterlist.

_____ 3. Using my list of positive traits (appendix B), I identified those most fitting to use in my summary statement(s) and cover letter(s). I confirmed that I can support these traits with material in my résumé.

_____ 4. I reviewed sample résumés (appendix G) to see which style/form (paragraph or bulleted) is best suited to the types and number of entries in my own résumé.

_____ 5. I drafted a résumé with my basic headings and information.

_____ 6. I used appendix C to draft a persuasive summary statement.

_____ 7. Using the list of action verbs (appendix D), I fine-tuned the prose that will be listed by bullet point/paragraph under my main headings.

_____ 8. I reviewed the sample résumé entry edits (appendix E) and edited my résumé accordingly.

_____ 9. I proofed my résumé for common grammatical errors (appendix F) and had at least two other persons carefully review it (chapter 5) as well.

_____ 10. I identified my references and gathered all pertinent information needed to provide their information upon request (chapter 6).

_____ 11. I read the sample cover letters (appendix G) and drafted one, using the guidelines of the appendices and the principles in chapter 6.

_____ 12. I checked my attitude to ensure that I am positive about myself and the job-search process.

Appendix H

KEY RÉSUMÉ-WRITING STEPS

Step 1 — Check your attitude

Step 2 — Create your Masterlist

Step 3 — Identify your skills, knowledge, and traits

Step 4 — Organize your content

Step 5 — Format your entries

Step 6 — Write your summary

Determine career-specific language

Step 7 — Edit résumé entries

Step 8 — Recruit your references

Step 9 — Draft a cover letter

Works Cited

Amare, Nicole, and Alan Manning. "Writing for the Robot: How Employer Search Tools Have Influenced Résumé Rhetoric and Ethics." *Business Communication Quarterly* 72 (2009): 35–60.

Applegate, Rachel. "Resumes and Cover Letters [For Library Employment]." *Indiana Libraries* 28 (2009): 28–35.

Barr, Terri Feldman, and Kevin M. McNeilly. "The Value of Students' Classroom Experiences from the Eyes of the Recruiter: Information, Implications, and Recommendations for Marketing Educators." *Journal of Marketing Education* 24 (2002): 168–173.

Beene, Ryan. "Cover Letter Perfect: Professionals Re-Entering the Job Market Need to Relearn Application Basics." *Crain's Detroit Business*, March 9, 2009, 9.

Bennet, Bo. *Year to Success.* Sudbury, MA: Archieboy Holdings, LLC, 2004.

Bennett, Scott. *The Elements of Résumé Style: Essential Rules and Eye-Opening Advice for Writing Résumés and Cover Letters that Work.* NY: AMACOM, 2005.

Blackburn-Brockman, Elizabeth, and Kelly Belanger. "One Page or Two?: A National Study of CPA Recruiters' Preferences for Résumé Length." *The Journal of Business Communication* 38 (2001): 29–57.

Block, Jay A. *101 Best Ways to Land a Job in Troubled Times.* NY: McGraw-Hill, 2009.

Bohnert, Daniel, and William H. Ross. "The Influence of Social Networking Web Sites on the Evaluation of Job Candidates." *Cyberpsychology, Behavior, and Social Networking* 13, forthcoming.

Bolles, Richard Nelson. *What Color Is Your Parachute?* 2009 ed. Berkeley, CA: Ten Speed Press, 2009.

Bright, Jim, and Joanne Earl. *Brilliant CV: What Employers Want to See and How to Say It.* Old Tappan, NJ: Prentice Hall, 2001.

Brown, Douglas J., Richard T. Cober, Kevin Kane, Paul E. Levy, and Jarret Shalhoop. "Proactive Personality and the Successful Job Search: A Field Investigation with College Graduates." *Journal of Applied Psychology* 91 (2006): 717–726.

Bryen, Diane Nelson, Blyden B. Potts, and Allison C. Carey. "So You Want to Work? What Employers Say about Job Skills, Recruitment and Hiring Employees Who Rely on AAC." *Augmentative and Alternative Communication* 22 (2007): 126–139.

"Cal State University at Northridge Professor Offers Tips for Updating Your Resume." *AScribe Business & Economics News Service.* September 9, 2005.

Crosby, Olivia. "Résumés, Applications, and Cover Letters." *Occupational Outlook Quarterly* 53 (2009): 18–29.

Culwell-Block, Beverly, and Jean Anna Sellers. "Résumé Content and Format—Do the Authorities Agree?" *Bulletin of the Association for Business Communication,* 57 (1994): 27–30.

Davis, Barbara D., and Clive Muir. "Résumé Writing and the Minority Student." *Business Communication Quarterly* 66 (2003): 39–51.

DeKay, Sam H. "Expressing Emotion in Electronic Job Cover Letters." *Business Communication Quarterly* 69 (2006): 435–439.

Foster, Helen. "A Visual Heuristic for Promoting a Rhetorically Based Job Search." *Business Communication Quarterly* 60 (1997): 163–165.

Freedman, David H. "The Monster Dilemma: Posting Jobs on the Web Is Easy; It's Sifting through Hundreds of Resumés That's a Pain." *Inc. Magazine,* May 2007, 77–78.

Freedman, Toby. *Career Opportunities in Biotechnology and Drug Development.* Cold Spring Harbor, NY: Cold Spring Harbor Laboratory Press, 2008.

Graham, Brian. *Get Hired Fast: Tap the Hidden Job Market in 15 Days.* Avon, MA: Adams Media, 2005.

Hattersley, Michael E. "Writing the Perfect Cover Letter: Strategies for Nailing Your Dream Job." *Harvard Management Communication Letter* 2 (1999): 4–5.

Hayden, D.A., and Michael Wilder. *From B.A. to Payday: Launching Your Career After College.* NY: Stewart, Tabori & Chang, 2008.

Howell, Sue. "Resume Do's and Don'ts." *Nursing* 39 (2009): 20–21.

Hutchinson, Kevin L., and Diane S. Brefka. "Personnel Administrators' Preferences for Résumé Content: Ten Years After." *Business Communication Quarterly* 60 (1997): 67–75.

Jansen, Julie. *I Don't Know What I Want, But I Know It's Not This: A Step-by-Step Guide to Finding Gratifying Work.* Rev. ed. NY: Penguin, 2010.

Jones, Stephen. "How to Create a Winning Resume." *The Black Collegian*, October 2007, 54-56.

Kay, Andrea. *Work's a Bitch and Then You Make It Work: 6 Steps to Go from Pissed Off to Powerful.* NY: Stewart, Tabori & Chang, 2009.

Larsen, Holly. "Getting Past the Screens: Recruiters Talk about Resume Strategies." *The Scientist* (19): S32–33.

Levinson, Jay Conrad, and David E. Perry. *Guerrilla Marketing for Job Hunters 2.0: 1,001 Unconventional Tips, Ticks, and Tactics for Landing Your Dream Job.* Hoboken, NJ: Wiley, 2009.

Levit, Alexandra. *They Don't Teach Corporate in College: A Twenty-Something's Guide to the Business World.* Rev. ed. Franklin Lakes, NJ: The Career Press, 2009.

Lore, Nicholas. *Now What? The Young Person's Guide to Choosing the Perfect Career.* NY: Fireside, 2008.

Miller, Dan. *48 Days to the Work You Love.* Rev. ed. Nashville: B & H Publishing, 2010.

Myers, Ford R. *Get the Job You Want, Even When No One's Hiring: Take Charge of Your Career, Find a Job You Love, and Earn What you Deserve.* Hoboken, NJ: Wiley, 2009.

Newlen, Robert R. *Resume Writing and Interviewing Techniques That Work! A How-to-Do-It Manual for Librarians.* NY: Neal-Schuman, 2006.

Pollak, Lindsey. *Getting from College to Career: 90 Things to Do Before You Join the Real World.* NY: Harper, 2007.

Ross, Craig M., and Sarah J. Young. "Résumé Preferences: Is It Really 'Business as Usual'?" *Journal of Career Development* 32 (2005): 153–164.

Rowh, Mark. "Building an E-Portfolio." *Career World*, November-December 2008, 26–28.

Saks, Alan M. "Multiple Predictors and Criteria of Job Search Success." *Journal of Vocational Behavior* 68, (2006): 400–415.

Schullery, Nancy M., Linda Ickes, and Stephen E. Schullery. "Employer Preferences for Résumés and Cover Letters." *Business Communication Quarterly* 72 (2009): 163–176.

Smart, Karl L. "Articulating Skills in the Job Search: Proving by Example." *Business Communication Quarterly* 67, (2004): 198–205.

Spinks, Nelda, and Barron Wells. "Are Preferences of Small Companies Likely to Agree with Those of Large Corporations Concerning Résumés and Application Letters?" *The Bulletin of the Association for Business Communication,* 56 (1993): 28–29.

Stevenson, Betsey. "The Internet and Job Search" (working paper, The Wharton School, The University of Pennsylvania, October 2008).

Thoms, Peg, Rosemary McMasters, Melissa R. Roberts, and Douglas A. Dombkowski. "Resume Characteristics as Predictors of an Invitation to Interview." *Journal of Business and Psychology* 13 (1999): 339–356.

Turner, Lance. "From 'The Ladder': Tips for Resume Writing." *Arkansas Business,* December 15, 2008, 19.

Vogt, Peter. *Career Wisdom for College Students: Insights You Won't Get in Class, on the Internet, or from Your Parents.* NY: Checkmark Books, 2007.

Whitten, Neal. "Jaw-Dropping Résumés." *PM Network* 19 (November 2005): 25.

Wood, Jennifer L., and James M. Schmidtke. "Lying on Job Applications: The Effects of Job Relevance, Commission, and Human Resource Management Experience." *Journal of Business and Psychology* 22 (2007): 1–9.

Index

CPSIA information can be obtained at www.ICGtesting.com
Printed in the USA
LVOW012013010112

261902LV00014B/69/P